TWAYNE'S WORLD AUTHORS SERIES
A Survey of the World's Literature

FRANCE

Maxwell A. Smith, Guerry Professor of French, Emeritus
The University of Chattanooga
Former Visiting Professor in Modern Languages
The Florida State University

EDITOR

Marcel Proust

TWAS 404

Marcel Proust

MARCEL PROUST

By PATRICK BRADY
Rice University

TWAYNE PUBLISHERS
A DIVISION OF G. K. HALL & CO., BOSTON

Library of Congress Cataloging in Publication Data

Brady, Patrick.
  Marcel Proust.

  (Twayne's world authors series ; TWAS 404 : France)
  Bibliography: p. 159 - 63.
  Includes index.
  1.   Proust, Marcel, 1871 - 1922—Criticism and interpretation.
PQ2631.R63Z545456   843'.9'12   77-6303
ISBN 0-8057-6307-4

MANUFACTURED IN THE UNITED STATES OF AMERICA

To my mother,
Frances Minahan Brady,
whose sensitive reading first inspired
my lasting love for great literature,
I fondly dedicate
this little book

Contents

About the Author

Patrick Brady has taught at the Universities of Lille, Melbourne, and Queensland and at Florida State, Rice, and Harvard Universities. He has written on literary theory and critical methodology, textual analysis, and the relationship between the arts, especially in connection with late-19th-century Impressionism and early-18th-century Rococo style.

Professor Brady's published works include *"L'Oeuvre" d'Emile Zola, roman sur les arts: manifeste, autobiographie, roman à clef* (Genève: Droz, 1967), *Structuralist Perspectives in Criticism of Fiction: Essays on* Manon Lescaut *and* La Vie de Marianne (Bern: Lang, 1977), *Le Bouc émissaire chez Emile Zola: Analyses structurales et sémiotiques de "Germinal" et de "L'Oeuvre"* (Paris: Klincksieck, 1978), and *Le Style rococo: Etat des recherches et perspectives critiques* (Paris: Jean-Michel Place [Coll. "Oeuvres et critiques"], forthcoming).

Preface

Marcel Proust objected to Sainte-Beuve's biographical approach to criticism because it confuses the writer as moral and social being with the writer as author. Loath to do Proust himself the disservice he felt Sainte-Beuve did to earlier writers, I shall interest myself here less in Proust than in the Proustian text. Evocation of the traditional historical-biographical perspective will be limited to a brief chronology preceding our text proper and a terminal chapter.

The choice of this textual perspective inevitably affects the interpretation of certain aspects of the work, and notably of a certain number of inconsistencies or even contradictions. Thus the last volume, entitled *Time Recaptured (Le Temps retrouvé)*, both provides a theory for the interpretation of the whole work and criticizes the crudeness of works that contain theory. An author-oriented perspective might attempt to resolve this contradiction by pointing out that the later parts of *Remembrance of Things Past (A la recherche du temps perdu)*[1] were not revised by Proust himself and were published after his death, so that contradictions like the one here in question should be seen as reflections of the unfinished state of the text. Such a perspective is, of course, conjectural, and tends to elude the problem by "explaining *away*" such aspects of the text (instead of "explaining" them, as I believe should be done, by application of the reader perspective). Moreover, it is inapplicable to earlier parts of the text, which also contain inner contradictions—between, for example, complaints of the impossibility of communication between the Self and external reality and demonstrations that such communication is entirely possible. My approach, then, will be reader-oriented and essentially immanent.

The present study presents new postulates for the interpretation of the basic features of the Proustian universe. In essence, these postulates are: that the "hidden meaning" of such elements as the trees, farms, and bell-towers is never explicitly revealed in the text and remains for the reader (or critic) to discover by close reading, deduction, and extrapolation (this is directly implied by the text itself, in its rejection of works which contain their own theory); and that the explicative theory provided here, which is based on a new study of the psychological condition of the fictional narrator (or at least of his younger self, whom we shall call "the protagonist"), is strongly supported by the fact that it brings together two apparently unrelated aspects of the Proustian text, namely, the triadic character of the groups of objects just mentioned and the symbiotic relationship between the narrator and his mother. In my opinion, these hitherto relatively neglected elements are of central importance to any in-depth interpretation of the *Recherche*.

The ideological approaches associated with the *Nouvelle Critique* (not to be confused with Anglo-American New Criticism) have been excluded. It is true that a Jungian interpretation, for example, of the *Recherche* is very tempting, with Morel as the Shadow or "dark brother" and Saint-Loup possibly as positive Shadow, a functional psychological categorization further supported by the explicitly symbolic color of the hair of these two characters. The protagonist's relationship with his mother is so symbiotic that he is unable to transfer his *anima* from her to another love-object (for example, Albertine); as a result, individuation does not occur. Moreover, the Wise Old Man is no doubt either Swann or Charlus, neither of whom plays the role particularly well—a circumstance which further inhibits individuation. It was felt, however, that approaches of this type, whether Jungian, Freudian, Marxist, or structuralist, were not appropriate to the present project.

To ensure that this study be useful to students and teachers of French, the location of all passages of the *Recherche* either quoted or mentioned is given both in the official English translation by C. K. Scott Moncrieff and in the French Pléiade edition (the latter reference follows the former in parenthesis on each occasion). While all quotations are given in English, essentially from the Scott Moncrieff translation, the entire study is based on the French of the Pléiade edition. This was made necessary both by the discrepancies between the two texts (for example, some passages which occur in the text of Scott Moncrieff [1924 - 1930] are relegated to footnotes in the Pléiade [1954]; the latter introduces totally new passages; and so on) and by the stylistic alterations caused by, or at least concomitant with, the process of translation (for example, the translation of a particular French word by several different English words in different contexts, which dilutes the stylistic effect of repetition).

The present study was undertaken with the conviction that the aims of a series like the Twayne World Authors are best served by essays which combine review and synthesis with critical innovation.

Preface

As for the simplicity of language required by the series, it has always been the present writer's belief that critical writing should be aimed primarily at communication, whose goals are best served by simplicity and clarity, however unfashionable such qualities may at times become. Whether these goals have been achieved, the reader himself must decide.

Grateful acknowledgment is made to the editors of *Neophilologus*, in whose pages one of these chapters originally appeared, for permission to reprint.

PATRICK BRADY

Rice University

Chronology

1871   July 10, Marcel Proust born in Paris.

1880   First attack of asthma.

1882   Enters the Lycée Condorcet. Studies under Gaucher (rhetoric) and Darlu (philosophy). Prize for philosophy in his final year (1889). During this period he contributes to the school magazine *(La Revue lilas)*, begins to frequent the fashionable *salons*.

1889-   Military service at Orléans. In the latter year enters the
1890   Ecole des Sciences Politiques.

1892   Literary debut in the review *Le Banquet*.

1893   Contributes to *Le Banquet* and *La Revue blanche*.

1894   Spends summer vacation at Trouville.

1895   Passes the entrance examination for the Bibliothèque Mazarine. Travels in Brittany with Reynaldo Hahn. Death of his maternal grandmother.

1895-   Writes *Jean Santeuil*. Avidly follows the Dreyfus case.
1899

1896   Publishes *Les Plaisirs et les jours* (reproducing articles published in *Le Banquet)* and *Portraits de peintres*.

1897   Duel with Jean Lorrain.

1899   Begins translation of Ruskin. Stay at Evian.

1900   Publishes first articles on Ruskin. Travels with his mother to Venice.

1903   Death of his father.

1903-   Articles on high society. In the latter year publishes *La*
1904   *Bible d'Amiens* (a translation of Ruskin).

1905   Death of his mother. Stay in clinic.

1906   Settles at 102 boulevard Haussmann; has his bedroom lined with cork. Publishes *Sésame et les lys* (a translation of Ruskin).

1907   Summer vacation at Cabourg. Automobile excursions in Normandy with his chauffeur Agostinelli. Probable beginning of the *Recherche (Remembrance of Things Past)*.

1909   Abandons social life to devote himself to the *Recherche*.

1910   Goes to see the Ballets russes. Summer vacation at Cabourg.
1912   Publishes extracts from the *Recherche* in *Le Figaro*. Makes Agostinelli his secretary.
1913   Tries in vain to have the *Recherche* published by Fasquelle, the Nouvelle Revue Française, Ollendorff. Employs Céleste Albaret. Publishes *Du côté de chez Swann (Swann's Way)* at his own expense.
1914   Article by Henri Ghéon on *Du côté de chez Swann*. Death of Agostinelli in an air crash. Publication of extracts of the *Recherche* in *La Nouvelle Revue Française*. Stay at Cabourg.
1918   Publishes *A l'ombre des jeunes filles en fleurs (Within a Budding Grove)*.
1919   Changes lodgings twice. Prix Goncourt awarded for *A l'ombre des jeunes filles en fleurs*. Publishes *Pastiches et mélanges*, incorporating articles published since 1904 (mainly in *Le Figaro*).
1920   *Le Côté de Guermantes (The Guermantes Way)*, I - II and *Sodome et Gomorrhe (Cities of the Plain)*, I.
1921   *Les Plaisirs et les jours*. Taken ill during visit to an exhibition of Dutch painting at the Musée du Jeu de Paume.
1922   *Sodome et Gomorrhe* II. Death of Marcel Proust.
1923   *La Prisonnière (The Captive)*.
1925   *Albertine disparue*, later entitled *La Fugitive (The Sweet Cheat Gone)*.
1927   *Le Temps retrouvé (The Past Recaptured)*, completing the publication of the *Recherche*.
1952   *Jean Santeuil*.

CHAPTER 1

A *Locus, a Voice, a Tone*

I *Point of View*

IT is impossible to attach too much importance to the fact that the whole of the *Recherche* is written in the first person.[1] This means that statements made without specific attribution must be attributed not to Proust the man nor even to Proust the author but to the fictional narrator. Their form and content thus contribute primarily to the gradual emergence of a self-portrait (conscious or unconscious) of this narrator. Moreover, portraits of others and accounts of events are—at least in part—voluntary creations of this narrator, and therefore rather to be taken as evidence of his private or fictional universe than as descriptions of any external reality, whether objectively or subjectively observed; indeed, the narrator himself constantly questions the very possibility of "objective" observation.

This view of the status of the text would be necessary even if the text itself contained no references to the question. As it happens, such references do occur, thus reinforcing the point we are making. Some are explicit but indirect: "Man is the creature that cannot emerge from himself, that knows his fellows only in himself; when he asserts the contrary, he is lying."[2] Others are more direct. Teasing reference is made to the narrator's name, which however is not revealed.[3] The narrator plays with the reader who is misguided enough to identify him with the author: " . . . she said: 'My ———' or 'My dearest ———' followed by my Christian name, which, if we were to give the narrator the same name as the author of this book, would have made: 'My Marcel,' or 'My dearest Marcel.' "[4] Both the implicit reminder that the narrator need *not* be given the same name as the author, and the use of the verb tense "would have made" *(eût fait)* indicate that "Marcel" is not (necessarily) the real name of the narrator.

However, apparently amused at the possibility of confusing the reader, and in any case having given this disclaimer as a caution, he then proceeds to use the same name on a later occasion (presumably with the assumption that he does not have to repeat the disclaimer): " 'My darling, dear Marcel. . . . What a Marcel! What a Marcel!' "[5] Several further references are made to the narrator's name—his last name this time. One occurs when he remarks that M. de Guermantes "gave M. d'Agrigente my name."[6] Another involves a telegram he receives: "The porter handed me a telegram which the messenger had already brought three times to the hotel, for owing to the inaccurate rendering of the recipient's name (which I recognized nevertheless, through the corruptions introduced by Italian clerks, as my own) the post-office required a signed receipt certifying that the telegram was addressed to myself."[7] Yet another is a reference not to written but to spoken language: "They [the servants] had whispered my name to one another and 'in their language,' one lady told how she had heard them say, 'There's Papa ———,' mentioning my name."[8] The suppression of the name is obvious in each of these cases, and especially in the last.

Even the apparently false first name is introduced long after we first began wondering what the narrator's name is and then came to presume that we should never be given it. Such procedures on the part of the narrator are often mirrored in the actions of other characters. Thus, we learn the first name of M. Verdurin the same way: " 'For he is as fond of you as I am, is Gustave' (from this we learned that M. Verdurin's name was Gustave)."[9] Another example: our narrator gives to the women in his life names which are as well or better known in their masculine form: "Gilberte," "Andrée," "Albertine," and consequently one cannot but wonder if he is playing with us again when he explicitly remarks of M. de Vaugoubert: "He gave all the men's names in the feminine and, as he was very stupid, he imagined this pleasantry to be extremely witty, and was continually in fits of laughter."[10]

It is clear that the narrator is very conscious of his relationship with the reader: "My words, therefore, did not in the least reflect my sentiments. If the reader has no more than a faint impression of these, that is because, as narrator, I reveal my sentiments to him at the same time as I repeat my words."[11] Sometimes this problem is approached even more explicitly by a direct statement to the reader: " 'I forget whether I mentioned . . . ,' I could appeal to the reader, as to a friend with regard to whom one completely forgets, at the end of a conversation, whether one has remembered, or had an opportunity to tell him something important."[12] At times, the narrator even invents an intervention on the part of the reader: " 'All this,' the reader will remark, 'tells us nothing. . . . ' No, but be quiet and let me go on with my story."[13] In such a case, of course, "the reader" is a pseudoreader invented by the narrator, the supposed intervention being placed in the mouth of a character created by (and therefore even more fictitious than) the narrator himself.

Various techniques are used to suggest the "veracity" of the narrative. Perhaps the most significant is that which admits to a very partial presentation of reality. "In the case of Albertine, the prospect of her continued society was painful to me in another fashion which I cannot explain in this narrative."[14] Sometimes this realistic inadequacy of the narration will be attributed to a failure to hear words accurately: "M. Verdurin added an expression. . . . But it cannot have been reported to me correctly, for it was not a French expression. . . ."[15] And again: ". . . the answer which she made me with an air of disgust and the exact words to tell the truth I could not make out (even the opening words, for she did not finish her sentence). I succeeded in establishing them only a little later when I had guessed what was in her mind."[16] But the purely technical character of such passages as these is indicated by the narrator's frequent references to the protagonist's "fictioneering," now around Albertine, now around "Mlle d'Eporcheville." He stresses the contrast between this taste for inventing and the observation of reality: ". . . what it tortured me to imagine in Albertine was my own perpetual desire to find favour with fresh ladies, to plan fresh romances. . . . Observation counts for little."[17]

This disclaimer as to any capacity for objective observation occurs several times, but should not be interpreted as modesty, for the "novelist-observer" is treated quite ironically by our narrator. As a result, he finds the lives of real people as vague as those of characters in a half-forgotten novel, and he insists on the purely fictional status of the events and characters included in his own narration. But the meaning of such declarations is clarified a few pages later, when he says that, although the writer must not "observe" and "take notes" deliberately, he inevitably draws, when writing, on a myriad of remembered details.

Perhaps the most remarkable instance of a play on reality and fiction is the rather moving passage in which he salutes "dear Charles Swann" and points out that he is only remembered and spoken of still because the narrator has made him the hero of a novel.

When we bring the implications of a first-person point of view to bear on the portrayal of surrogate selves such as Swann, we immediately perceive that thoughts and feelings imputed to such surrogates must be assumed to be, at best, second- or third-hand reports being retailed as fact or, at "worst," purely fictitious attributions (or even imaginings) on the part of the narrator. Sometimes the report given of another person is so internal to that character that we can be virtually certain that such information is not available to the narrator, as when he affirms of the young man named Octave that while he was intellectually null he was kept awake at night by the ineffectual itch to think. Such cases remind us forcibly of the degree of pure invention involved in a narrative of this type—not merely invention by the implied author (let alone Proust the man) but invention by an invented entity, namely, the fictional narrator. It is invention of the third degree.

A certain playing with time further reinforces this impression: "Indeed we may mention (to anticipate by a few weeks the narrative which we shall take up again immediately after this parenthesis which we open while M. de Charlus, Brichot and I are moving towards Mme Verdurin's house). . . ."[18] The suggestion here is that the parenthesis fills in a "real" lapse of time—but a moment's reflection enables us to see that the three characters cannot move forward toward Mme. Verdurin's house during the parenthesis except by implication, for their movement depends on its being described (that is, invented), either as occurring or as having occurred, by the narrator. The parenthesis therefore arrests the movement of the characters because it arrests the narration.

Finally, let us note that even so perceptive a protagonist at times appears surprisingly obtuse. Some passages indicate that when young he was capable of a selfishness which made him exceedingly insensitive (or stupid)—as he regrets later: the narrator evokes "the astonishment, I might almost say the shame that I felt at never having even once told myself that Albertine, in my house, was in a false position, which might give offence to her aunt."[19] Others suggest that he was blind to the nature of his own feelings: "Albeit I did not believe in friendship, nor did I believe that I had ever felt any real friendship for Robert, when I thought about those stories of the lift-boy and of the restaurant in which I had had luncheon with Saint-

Loup and Rachel, I was obliged to make an effort to restrain my tears."[20] And although he sometimes prefers to doubt things he does not want to believe (such as the final portrait of Albertine drawn by Aimé and Andrée), he is often tempted to believe totally the last version of a story he is told by some informant apparently just because it comes later than other versions.

II   *The Difficulty of Interpretation*

The language of interpretation recurs frequently—either in such phrases as "visible characters," "tiny red cuneiform hieroglyphs," "superimposed symbols," or in the many references to systems of *signs*. Errors in comprehension and interpretation may be caused by the impassable walls of the Self, by the difficulties inherent in communication, by the complexity of reality (of a person, for example), by the masks and roles afforded (or imposed) by affectation and snobbery, or by the use of deliberate concealment or deceit.

The feeling that the walls of the Self are impassable is reflected in the definition of Reality as "everything which was not myself," and frustration resulting from this feeling is clearly affirmed: "Hardly even does one think of oneself, but only how to escape from oneself."[21] On the other hand, many elements strongly suggest that the narrating consciousness, if it never escapes from the prism of its Self, does enter into other objects and sensibilities: certain episodes suggest that things and literary characters may interpenetrate, as the magic-lantern figure of Golo absorbs the bedroom doorhandle, and are interchangeable, like the mobile bell-towers of Vieuxvicq and Martinville.

Certain misunderstandings result from the difficulties and obstacles inherent in all communication, as we see from episodes concerning the narrator's bachelor uncle and a neighbor, Legrandin. The first of these is rather sad: the protagonist reports to his parents his meeting with a strangely charming young woman at his uncle's place, thinking they will be as interested and delighted as he—the first misconstruction; then he avoids raising his hat to his uncle because of the inadequacy of such a means of communication to convey his feelings of warmth and distress—a nongesture which is tragically misinterpreted by the uncle as a rejection of him. In the case of Legrandin, the family's conviction that he is simple and unpretentious prevents them from accepting a new image of him as a snob and hypocrite, even though this view is the more accurate.

Reality may defy comprehension by its very complexity. Reality *as known* consists of our sensations and perceptions: the protagonist's inability to penetrate his own sensations of pleasure at certain visual experiences is emphasized, as is the common phenomenon of people's blindness to the complexity of people they meet, such as Legrandin, whose snobbery makes of him a hypocrite and a liar; Vinteuil, whose modesty hides his genius; or Swann, whose discretion conceals his distinguished relations. When he discovers what Françoise has (allegedly) been saying about him behind his back, he reflects in surprise: "A person does not (as I had imagined) stand motionless and clear before our eyes . . . but is a shadow which we can never succeed in penetrating, of which there can be no such thing as direct knowledge."[22] Lying, habitual to Albertine for example, complicates our arrival at the truth. Andrée is even more complex: she has a surface nature full of kindness and delicate attentions, a deeper level marked by envy and pride, and a third, even deeper nature, still partly at the potential stage, which tends toward goodness and the love of her neighbor.

The penultimate volume, *The Sweet Cheat Gone (La Fugitive)*, presents a series of startling revelations regarding Albertine. The first is the story told (allegedly) by the shower-girl to Aimé, revealing that Albertine was in the habit of closeting herself for long periods of time in a shower-bath with various women, including "a tall woman older than herself, always dressed in grey" and "a woman with a very dark skin and long-handled glasses" but consisting mainly of "girls younger than herself, especially one with a high complexion."[23] Then a young laundress makes (allegedly) a second revelation to Aimé about her lesbian relations with Albertine and other girls at the seaside, and finally an even more striking revelation about Albertine is made directly to the narrator by Andrée, who claims not only to have had a lesbian relationship with her friend but also that Albertine and Morel collaborated in corrupting young girls whom they led, by persuasion and by pressure, from heterosexuality to homosexuality to promiscuous lesbianism. This is, in fact, the most "sensational" passage of the *Recherche*.

A profound skepticism as to the reliability of appearances is expressed again and again: it is claimed, for example, that those who appear hard are weak people whom no one has wanted, while those who are really strong are not afraid to adopt a gentle manner which common people mistake for weakness. A striking image represents this deceptive character of what we see: "M. de Charlus lived in a state of deception like the fish which thinks that the water in which it is swimming extends beyond the glass wall of its aquarium which mirrors it."[24] The relations of Charlus with Morel are particularly characterized by misinterpretation: when Charlus catches Morel blushing out of embarrassment for the little clan, he interprets this sign of irritation and shame as pregnant with a very different meaning. The misunderstanding between the protagonist and Bloch is a typical example of misreading of appearances. Another fascinating scene of this type is that which takes place at the end of the Morel-Charlus soirée at the Verdurins' when Mme. de Valcourt misinterprets the glances of Mme. de Mortemart. Similar misunderstandings occur constantly between the protagonist and Albertine. And ignorance of the past leads new members of high society to make gross errors concerning the respective social distinction of Swann, Forcheville, and Saint-Loup.[25]

The difficulty of interpretation is conveyed through the provision of a cluster of possible alternatives. A typical example is the following concerning the liftboy (elevator operator): "He vouchsafed no answer, whether from astonishment at my words, preoccupation with what he was doing, regard for convention, hardness of hearing, respect for holy ground, fear of danger, slowness of understanding, or by the manager's orders."[26] In another passage, the narrator speculates on the reasons why the lord and lady of Féterne avoided inviting their well-born friends at the same time as the Verdurin group, attributing it to timidity (fear of annoying their noble friends), naivety (imagining M. and Mme. Verdurin might be bored with people who were not intellectuals), or lack of imagination (fear of committing a social blunder by mixing incompatible groups).[27] Similarly, many factors explain Charlus' tendency to lie, including the desire to appear natural and bold, the instinctive concealment of a secret rendezvous, the need to make known something agreeable and flattering to oneself, and so on.[28] Why do people invariably withhold information from a jealous lover?—no sooner is the question formulated than three possible reasons are immediately furnished.[29] After Albertine's death, the narrator reflects: "Perhaps my wealth, the prospect of a brilliant marriage had attracted her, my jealousy had kept her, her goodness or her intelligence, or her sense of guilt, or her cunning had made her accept, and had led me on to make harsher and harsher a captivity in chains forged simply by the internal process of my mental toil."[30]

III *Humour, Irony, Satire*

We are charmed and seduced by the manifestations of a delightful sense of humor which in the early part of the work is very gentle.
Thus he refers jokingly to the manner in which reality impinges on
the world of the magic lantern, describing the apparently
miraculous manner in which the body and even the facial expression of Golo "supernaturally" adapted themselves to the material
objects upon which they were projected, even down to the doorhandle, absorbing them without any visible effects of indigestion from
this transubstantiation. It is with sympathetic amusement that he
evokes his grandmother's "keen, jerky little step regulated by the
various effects wrought upon her soul by the intoxication of the
storm, the force of hygiene, the stupidity of my education and of
symmetry in gardens."[31] The scene in which the protagonist's great-
aunts attempt to thank Swann for his gift of wine is extremely com-
ical, their desire to be discreet being so strong that they limit
themselves to declarations that "M. Vinteuil is not the only one who
has nice neighbours" and "there are some days when I find reading
the papers very pleasant indeed, . . . when they write about
things or people in whom we are interested," enigmatic phrases accompanied by "significant glances."[32]

A mild irony creeps into his theory concerning the growing
deafness of his two great-aunts: their detachment from everything
relating to life in society was so complete that as soon as such
frivolous subjects were broached their auditory faculties simply
"turned off"—a habit which was gradually producing an effect of
atrophy. Sometimes the narrator's irony seems to be triggered by
irony on the part of one of his characters: when Aunt Flora evokes
the "charming" prospect of having a certain old gentleman talk to
them for hours on end about Maubant or about women's
cooperatives—" 'That must be delightful,' sighed my grandfather,
in whose mind nature had unfortunately forgotten to include any
capacity whatsoever for becoming passionately interested in the co-
operative movement among the ladies of Sweden or in the methods
employed by Maubant to get up his parts."[33]

Later in the work the purely comic scenes have a more farcical
flavor. One such concerns M. Nissim Bernard, an old Jewish
pederast, who makes an unfortunate choice of favorites: "This rubi-
cund youth, with his blunt features, appeared for all the world to
have a tomato instead of a head. A tomato exactly similar served as

head to his twin brother."[34] What complicates things is that the
twin likes only women, and as M. Bernard, who is short-sighted,
continually mistakes him for his brother, he is continually receiving
a black eye. In the end he becomes so disgusted with this that he
cannot stand either the boys or tomatoes. Another comic scene is
produced by the misleading appearance of Le Palace, a brothel
which looks like a luxury hotel; passengers arriving at Maineville by
train to visit Mme. Verdurin at Balbec invariably decide to stay
there: " 'There is the very thing I want. . . . I can tell at a glance
that it has all the modern comforts; I can quite well invite Mme
Verdurin there. . . . This seems to me the very place for her, and
for your wife, my dear Professor. There are bound to be sitting
rooms, we can have the ladies there. Between you and me, I can't
imagine why Mme Verdurin didn't come and settle here instead of
taking la Raspelière. . . . Mme Verdurin would have played the
hostess here to perfection.' "[35] And then there are the *pantalon-
nades* of Elstir in Mme. Verdurin's salon: he would send word at the
last moment that he could not come, then appear disguised as an
extra waiter and, as he passed around the dishes, whisper
obscenities to the prudish Mme. Putbus; then he would disappear
before the end of the dinner, and have brought into the living room
a bathtub full of water from which, at the end of the meal, he would
emerge stark naked and cursing loudly.

Ironic passages gradually become more biting and tend toward
satire. The narrator makes fun of Françoise and of "society" in the
same breath, when evoking her smiling acknowledgment of a very
weak joke she has not even understood: what made her happy was
the thought that it was for this sort of humor that people dressed up
and went out in the evening, at the risk of catching cold, even in the
highest society. M. de Charlus' extraordinary vanity leads him to
misinterpret his protégé's reactions: blind to Morel's sulky expression of silent displeasure at being taken back to Paris, he is per-
suaded that " 'he became wild with joy. . . . How proudly he
reared his head! . . . [He] was struck dumb with joy!' And M. de
Charlus (whom his joy, on the contrary, did not deprive of speech)
. . . cried out by himself and at the top of his voice raising his
hands in the air: 'Alleluia!' "[36]

Numerous satirical passages are devoted to the description of
Mme. Verdurin's affectation of laughter—we can quote only one of
them:

She would descend, with the suddenness of the insects called may-flies, upon Princess Sherbatoff; were the latter within reach the Mistress would cling to her shoulder, dig her nails into it, and hide her face against it for a few moments like a child playing at hide and seek. Concealed by this protecting screen, she was understood to be laughing until she cried and was as well able to think of nothing at all as people are who while saying a prayer that is rather long take the wise precaution of burying their faces in their hands. Mme Verdurin used to imitate them when she listened to Beethoven quartets, so as at the same time to let it be seen that she regarded them as a prayer and not to let it be seen that she was asleep.[37]

Sometimes the irony becomes quite ferocious: "[M. Verdurin] knew that a family doctor can do many little sevices, such as prescribing that one must not give way to grief. The docile Cottard had said to the Mistress: 'Upset yourself like that, and tomorrow you will *give me* a temperature of 102,' as he might have said to the cook: 'Tomorrow you will give me a *riz de veau.*' Medicine, when it fails to cure the sick, busies itself with changing the sense of verbs and pronouns."[38]

Ironic passages sometimes betray an interest in the manipulation of language. Examples include the merest drawing-room pun, like Oriane's joke about the general unlucky at politics whose wife becomes pregnant: "That's the one division where the poor General has never failed to get in."[39] More interesting is the passage representing the lesson of purely exterior humility and stupendous interior pride taught by her mother to the Princesse de Parme:

Remember that if God has caused you to be born on the steps of a throne you ought not to make that a reason for looking down upon those to whom Divine Providence has willed (wherefore His Name be praised) that you should be superior by birth and fortune. On the contrary, you must suffer the little ones. Your ancestors were Princes of Treves and Juliers from the year 647: God has decreed in His bounty that you should hold practically all the shares in the Suez Canal and three times as many Royal Dutch as Edmond de Rothschild; your pedigree in a direct line has been established by genealogists from the year 63 of the Christian Era; you have as sisters-in-law two Empresses. Therefore, never seem, in your speech, to be recalling these great privileges, not that they are precarious (for nothing can alter antiquity of race, while the world will always need petrol), but because it is useless to point out that you are better born than other people or that your investments are all gilt-edged, since everyone knows these facts already.[40]

The pleasure in playing with language is evident in the narrator's mock-heroic evocation of the telephone operators. Most frequently, however, this interest in the color provided by certain stylistic tones (and sometimes weaknesses) is expressed through language attributed to characters other than the narrator—the pseudo-Homeric language of Bloch (often interlarded with slang), the bombastic rhetoric of M. de Charlus, the pedantic elucubrations of Brichot, the stream of clichés uttered by M. de Norpois, on the one hand, and, on the other, the errors and malapropisms which characterize the language of Françoise and her young footman, the Duc de Guermantes, and members of the staff of the Grand Hôtel de Balbec such as the director and the liftboy. Bloch, for example, likes to express himself in the following manner: "Here is a book which I have not the time, just now, to read, a book recommended, it would seem, by that colossal fellow (my very dear master, Father Lecomte, who is found pleasing in the sight of the immortal gods). He regards, or so they tell me, its author, one Bergotte, Esquire, as a subtle scribe, more subtle, indeed, than any beast of the field; and, albeit he exhibits on occasion a critical pacifism, a tenderness in suffering fools, for which it is impossible to account, and hard to make allowance, still his word has weight with me as it were the Delphic Oracle. Read you then this lyrical prose, and, if the Titanic master-builder of rhythm who composed *Bhagavat* and the *Lévrier de Magnus* speaks not falsely, then, by Apollo, you may taste, even you, my master, the ambrosial joys of Olympus."[41]

The language of M. de Charlus is characterized above all by vanity and pride, which causes him to take special pleasure in being insulting and ironic: " 'Oh! Sir. . . . I think that you are doing yourself an injustice when you accuse yourself of having said that we were *friends*. I do not look for any great verbal accuracy in anyone who could readily mistake a piece of Chippendale for a rococo *chaire*, but really I do not believe . . . that you can ever have said, or thought, that we were *friends!* As for your having boasted that you had been *presented* to me, had *talked* to me, *knew* me slightly, had obtained, almost without solicitation, the prospect of coming one day under my *protection*, I find it on the contrary very natural and intelligent of you to have done so.' "[42] The "wit" of Brichot, like that of Cottard, is weak and laborious: "Maecenas interests me chiefly because he is the earliest apostle of note of that Chinese god who numbers more followers in France today than Brahma, than Christ himself, the all-powerful God Ubedamd."[43]

M. de Norpois is above all a specialist in clichés, as when he addresses Bloch:

I know that the Socialist Party are crying aloud for his head on a charger, as well as for the immediate release of the prisoner from the Devil's Isle. But I think that we are not yet reduced to the necessity of passing the Caudine Forks of MM. Gérault-Richard and Company. So far the whole case has been an utter mystery. . . . Should you retire to your tents and burn your boats, you would do so to your own damnation. . . . If you do not allow yourselves to be dragooned by the fishers in troubled waters, you will have won your battle. I do not guarantee that the whole of the General Staff is going to get away unscathed, but it will be so much to the good if some of them at least can save their faces without setting the heather on fire.[44]

IV *Inversion, Introversion, and the Failure to Consummate*

Inversion is a major theme of the work, a preoccupation which is reflected in the title of *Cities of the Plain (Sodome et Gomorrhe)*. Homosexuals of both sexes are portrayed: pederasts like M. de Charlus, Prince Gilbert de Guermantes, M. de Vaugoubert, Nissim Bernard, Legrandin, Robert de Saint-Loup, and the objects of their affection—Jupien, Morel, Theodore, and others; lesbians like Mlle. Vinteuil and her friend, Lea the actress, Bloch's cousin, probably Andrée, and Albertine.

This theme of inversion is explicitly related to that of introversion (a much more common and anodine psychological phenomenon, of course) in a passage in which Albertine indicates, "set in the wall in front of us, a large mirror which I had not noticed and upon which I now realised that my friend, while talking to me, had never ceased to fix her troubled, preoccupied eyes."[45] In this mirror Albertine has been exchanging glances with two lesbians. The essential character of homosexuality, moreover, is well symbolized by the mirror, for the invert is attracted by the alter ego character of the objects of his or her attention. The mirror also symbolizes mere introversion. There is not conclusive evidence that the protagonist is a homosexual, but inversion is closely related to introversion, and the narrator is certainly quite introverted. In spite of his active social life, he very often expresses a strong preference for solitude. It leads him to condemn friendship, whose whole aim, he asserts, is to get us to sacrifice to a superficial self the only *real* part of ourselves, which cannot be communicated except through art. He compares the temptation of friendship to that of a pointless cause for which an artist, afraid of seeming or possibly being selfish, gives his life instead of living for the masterpiece which he bears within him.

In such passages, the narrator is concerned with solitude as a condition for creativity: "Robert having finished giving his instructions to the driver joined me now in the carriage. The ideas that had appeared before me took flight. Ideas are goddesses who deign at times to make themselves visible to a solitary mortal, at a turning in the road, even in his bedroom while he sleeps, when they, standing framed in the doorway, bring him the annunciation of their tidings. But as soon as a companion joins him they vanish, in the society of his fellows no man has ever beheld them. And I found myself cast back upon friendship."[46] Like Robert de Saint-Loup, Albertine threatens the precious solitude of the protagonist: she is a perpetual presence, greedy for movement and life, which disturbs his sleep, ever leaving doors open for him to catch cold, and forcing him to invent reasons for not accompanying her on outings. In particular, her mere presence prevents him from experiencing certain pleasures: whereas she feels her pleasure at seeing certain monuments would be increased by seeing them with him, he believes he could neither give nor feel any pleasure at seeing them unless he visited them alone or at least pretended to be alone. Solitude is essential: "Albertine admired, and by her presence prevented me from admiring, the reflections of red sails upon the wintry blue of the water."[47] Thus the most precious of both active and passive functions, that is, of both artistic creation and aesthetic pleasure, are dependent, for the protagonist, on solitude.

To this theme of introversion we may relate that of narcissism, of which we need give only a partial indication at this point. He asserts that he is modest enough to seek to hide his good qualities, speaking of "the people in whose company I have succeeded in concealing most effectively the slight advantages a knowledge of which might have given them a less derogatory idea of myself";[48] later he claims to be so modest that he is not even aware of these qualities: "I realised that the Guermantes did indeed regard me as being of another race, but one that aroused their envy because I possessed merits of which I knew nothing and which they professed to regard as alone important."[49] The "insincerity" betrayed by the inconsistency between such statements is revealed on other occasions as well: after admitting that he is "the least courageous of men,"[50] he will later declare that, "I had never been timid, I had been easily led into duels,"[51] and denies any fear of the shells and bombs falling on Paris during World War I. A further inconsistency is associated with his grandmother. (It is in connection with her memory that he blames his symbiotic hypersensitivity for inspiring in him a cow-

ardly refusal to face cruelty and injustice.) He declares that like her
he is unable to judge others or bear grudges and is free from vanity
and pride, as from self-respect *(amour-propre)*, but his own self-
portrait betrays great vanity and pride (in the form of narcissism,
snobbery, and so on), and at least one important form of *amour-
propre* admitted to quite explicitly and at great length: that which
involves risking danger in order to retain another's high opinion of
him and of his noble and favorable disposition.

The theme of impotence is evoked in connection with M.
d'Argencourt, who abandons his wife for a young socialite but finds
her sexually difficult to satisfy. What of the protagonist himself? He
speaks several times of having possessed Albertine and of being her
lover—and indeed of having had other mistresses. In fact, he is inclined to boast of the number of his conquests: "I must confess that
many of her friends—I was not yet in love with her—gave me, at
one watering-place or another, moments of pleasure. These obliging
young comrades did not seem to me to be very many. But recently I
have thought it over, their names have recurred to me. I counted
that, in that one season, a dozen conferred on me their ephemeral
favours. A name came back to me later, which made thirteen. I
then, with almost a child's delight in cruelty, dwelt upon that
number. Alas, I realised that I had forgotten the first of them all,
Albertine who no longer existed and who made the fourteenth."[52]

Nevertheless, several indications suggest that intercourse is
beyond him, psychologically if not physically. The key passage here
is the following, which dilutes drastically the meaning to be attributed to the term "lover" claimed elsewhere by the narrator:
"Albertine alarmed me further when she said that I was quite right
to say, out of regard for her reputation, that I was not her lover,
since 'for that matter,' she went on, 'it's perfectly true that you
aren't.' I was not her lover perhaps in the full sense of the word, but
then, was I to suppose that all the things that we did together she
did also with all the other men whose mistress she swore to me that
she had never been?"[53] From this passage we may deduce that the
protagonist has not actually had sexual intercourse with Albertine.
Such a hypothesis would explain her desire for relations with a man,
as expressed in the exclamation "Thank you for nothing! Fancy
spending a cent upon those old frumps, I'd a great deal rather you
left me alone for once in a way so that I can go and get some one
decent to break my [pot]."[54] The narrator comments as follows:
"Horror! It was this that she would have preferred. Two-fold

horror! For even the vilest of prostitutes, who consents to that sort of thing, or desires it, does not employ to the man who yields to her desires that appalling expression. She would feel the degradation too great. To a woman alone, if she loves women, she says this, as an excuse for giving herself presently to a man."[55] It is striking that he twice describes his own orgasm, once with Gilberte and once with Albertine, but never that of his partner, who seems to be thus reduced (like the reader) to the role of spectator.

It is possible, on the other hand, that the protagonist, who is capable of orgasm and is therefore not really impotent, simply has no taste for the consummation of sexual relations with a woman—which brings us back to our starting point: inversion. Such a hypothesis would explain a number of other elements of the work, including the protagonist's striking resemblance with one of the female characters: "At that moment I caught sight of myself in the mirror; I was struck by a certain resemblance between myself and Andrée. If I had not long since ceased to shave my upper lip and had had but the faintest shadow of a moustache, the resemblance would have been almost complete."[56]

Another significant resemblance is that between the protagonist and M. de Charlus. If the latter is always on the side of the weak, so is the protagonist; the latter's identification of individuals with the village and the countryside to which they belong reappears in Charlus; the particular form of selfishness shown by the protagonist toward Albertine recurs in Charlus' treatment of Morel. And whereas there is some evidence, as I have indicated, that the protagonist may be psychologically incapable of intercourse (at least with women), Charlus is obsessed with a dream of virility. These resemblances would then explain the narrator's keen appreciation of Charlus. The most striking of them is the similarity between Charlus' relationship with his protégé (sketched with the protagonist and carried out with Morel) and the protagonist's relationship with his protégée Albertine. Other elements then come to mind: the fact that the protagonist's preference goes to a girl like Albertine, who first strikes him as athletic and is finally described as being "masculine"[57] and the counterpart of Charlus: "It was perhaps, I told myself, Albertine's vice itself, the cause of my future sufferings, that had produced in her that honest, frank manner, creating the illusion that one could enjoy with her the same loyal and unrestricted comradeship as with a man, just as a parallel vice had produced in M. de Charlus a feminine refinement of sensibility and mind."[58]

The protagonist reveals an apparent passivity in his physical relations with the opposite sex. Thus to express his desire for Albertine he invites her to tickle him! She will not let him kiss her except when, as he says, "it was I, now, who was lying in bed and she who sat beside me, capable of evading any brutal attack and of dictating her pleasure to me."[59] The transparent request to be tickled occurs again later, this time with a servant, whom he tells to search him (in the dark: he has blown out the candle) for money. His passivity with Albertine is fairly constant: generally, she controls the situation, whether preventing his action or taking the initiative herself. He experiences Albertine's kiss "like a penetration."[60]

To the narrator, with his passion for the study of abnormal psychological states, we may well apply his own comment: "What specialist in the insane has not, as a result of spending time with them, had his attack of insanity? In fact he is lucky if he can affirm that it was not a previous, latent insanity that had moved him to work with them. The object of a psychiatrist's studies often reacts on him. But before that, what obscure inclination, what fascinating fear had made him choose that object?"[61] It is true that he tries to persuade us that the abnormal psychology he studies is in fact normal, at least in the sense of being universal in human nature: "When a living being—and perhaps in nature that creature is man—is so poorly constituted that he cannot love without suffering and must suffer in order to learn new truths. . . ."[62] But this is not particularly persuasive.

His taste for little girls, which gets him into trouble with the police for corrupting a minor, is a pathetic way for him to end, with a request that Gilberte supply him with new ones; it tends to support the view that his own psychological makeup is something less than normal.

It is clear not only that the *Recherche* is a remarkable example of first-person narration, but also that this circumstance determines many basic aspects of the text. Thus the difficulty of interpretation is naturally emphasized by a narrator who sees only the Self as knowable; and the text is colored by the narrator's psychological and moral makeup—his sense of humor and satire, his introversion and probable inversion.

CHAPTER 2

Selves

I Sleep, Dreams, and the Divided Self

IN the course of the *Recherche* we are led through a remarkable gamut of shades of awareness and relationship, passing
from consciousness to self-awareness, awareness of reality, relation
to reality, incomprehension, concealment, misinterpretation, distor-
tion, invention, and identification.

The brief first sentence establishes the character of the discourse
which is beginning: being a first-person narration, this search for
lost time will be reported directly by the searcher, by an explorer of
the world, of the Other, and above all of the Self. For a wonderful
awareness of self colors every passage, beginning with—the beginning: "Sometimes, when I had put out my candle, my eyes would
close so quickly that I had not even time to say 'I'm going to sleep.'
And half an hour later the thought that it was time to go to sleep
would awaken me."[1]

The narrator explores the subtle refraction of the sense of self
through the twilight state between waking and sleeping. This confusion, which affects the self seeking to slip gradually from the waking into the sleeping state, is analogous to that which weighs on the
gradually awakening self. The portrayal of this type of theme is of
course easier to render when the subject of the process is the self,
for these sensations and impressions are very intimate in kind; but
there are some examples of others also concerning themselves with
preserving the sense of identity associated with the waking state and
threatened by sleeping. Thus the narrator writes of his Aunt Léonie:
"I would often hear her saying to herself: 'I must not forget that I
never slept a wink.' "[2] The interest of such passages is not merely
anecdotal: they are significant echoes, within the fictional elaboration, of some of his most intimate preoccupations. His struggle
against mortality and the passage of time, for instance, which con-

stitutes the underlying theme (and structure) of the whole work, finds implicit expression in this otherwise parasitic evocation of the old lady's struggle against the "little death" of sleep.

Many pages of the *Recherche* are devoted to describing the state of sleep, usually that of the protagonist, which reduces the individuality of the sleeper: "One is no longer a person"[3]—passages in the course of which he contests Bergson's view of the effect of drugs on the memory. The narrator speaks of "that deep slumber in which are opened to us a return to childhood, the recapture of past years, of lost feelings, the disincarnation, the transmigration of the soul, the evoking of the dead, the illusions of madness, retrogression towards the most elementary of the natural kingdoms . . . , all those mysteries which we imagine ourselves not to know and into which we are in reality initiated almost every night, as we are into the other great mystery of annihilation and resurrection."[4] He also describes the sleep of Albertine. In the oyster of sleep, there sometimes develops that strange pearl which we call a dream: several of the protagonist's dreams are described, especially those devoted to his dead grandmother—who, interestingly enough, is associated each time with his father. Other dreams evoked are the nightmares that torment Saint-Loup or Bergotte and a vivid dream of Swann's involving Odette, himself, and "a young man in a fez whom he failed to identify":[5] "The young man whom he had failed, at first, to identify, was himself also; like certain novelists, he had distributed his own personality between two characters, him who was the 'first person' in the dream, and another whom he saw before him, capped with a fez"[6]—an image of the roles of protagonist and Swann in the *Recherche* itself.

This division of the personality is also reflected elsewhere. We find it evoked in connection with actors, in the temporal sequence of different Albertines and protagonists, and above all in the division of the self. The narrator remarks of the pleasures of the *tutoiement* (the familiar or intimate form of address) of Gilberte: "They were given, not by the little girl whom I loved, to me who loved her, but by the other, her with whom I used to play, to my other self."[7] Sometimes the narrator draws aside and views his younger self, the protagonist of his story, with ironic detachment. At other times, the protagonist seems to experience within himself a painful division of personality: "The first instant I angrily asked myself who was the stranger that came thus to cause me pain, and that stranger was my own self, the child I had been in those days."[8] One such passage has a vivid reminiscence of Marivaux and Pascal: "I say my reason, not myself."[9] One of the most striking examples of division of self is the following passage: "It is when we are ill that we realize that we do not live alone, but chained to a being belonging to a different realm, separated from us by abysses, which does not know us and to which it is impossible for us to make ourselves understood: our body."[10]

The division of the self is produced by growing awareness: awareness of sensations (and thus of existence and the fact of sensation), awareness of the coherence and cohesion of these sensations (and thus of the existence of a sensing self), and awareness of the sources of these sensations (and thus of "external" reality, at least as a hypothesis). The latter two stages show the internal division of the self (as the self observes itself) and its division or separation from reality.

As we read, we are gradually drawn into the intimacy of the narrator's personality through his sensitivity and his wealth of association. His own body is a space and time machine by which (or by whose sense-impressions) he is transported through time to other places strung—like photographic prints still wet and blurry, pegged to a line and left to dry—along that linear continuum which is constituted by the residues of his life. We are carried in rapid succession from bed to deserted countryside to strange hotel; we identify with homesick traveler and sleepless invalid; we fluctuate between childhood and later periods spent at Balbec, Paris, Venice, and other places; until at last we are set down at Combray, which will therefore be the first of these places we are to know in any detail.

II　*Self-Portrayal*

The features of the protagonist's character as the narrator describes it to us may be classified as positive (qualities), negative (defects), and neutral. The first two of these categories are dealt with elsewhere; here we shall deal only with the third, involving such features as sensitivity, introversion, passivity, illness, and so on.

Literature is full of "sacred wounds" which signify that the sufferer is marked for a special fate, often for a special role of seer, revealer, or mere bearer or symbol, of hidden truths. (The mutilation so often associated with initiation rites is connected with this conception.) Such is the limp inflicted on Sophocles' Oedipus or Zola's Gervaise or Jeanlin, the physical blindness of Tiresias (and ul-

timately of Oedipus); and such is the vague and mysterious illness
which afflicts the protagonist of the *Recherche*. As a result, the image of a suffering invalid comes readily to the narrator's mind; he
dwells on his Aunt Léonie's illness and that of his grandmother; and
his own is evoked almost continually throughout the work.

He is evidently extremely emotional and inclined to weep, as
shown in his reactions to his great-aunt's cruelty, M. de Norpois,
Saint-Loup's commanding officer, his grandmother's doctor, the
absence of a mistress, his own letter to Albertine, or the revelation
of Saint-Loup's deceptions. He compares himself to a plant, to a
flower, and this type of image provides a striking description (and
defense) of introversion: "We are not like buildings to which stones
can be added from without, but like trees which draw from their
own sap the knot that duly appears on their trunks, the spreading
roof of their foliage."[11] This is a restatement of the earlier comment
on "the selfish, active, practical, mechanical, indolent, centrifugal
tendency which is that of the human mind."[12] The protagonist is
described as having a constitution in which the nerves perform their
functions poorly, failing to prevent the arrival at the conscious level
of the painful and exhausting complaint of the humblest elements
of the self which are about to disappear. Andrée is described as
resembling the protagonist because of her neurotic makeup—excessively intellectual, nervous, and sickly.

In spite of his intelligence and sensitivity, the narrator's younger
self at times appears rather naive: he is surprised to find that the
compliments he pays Albertine are not a source of particular
pleasure to her best friend. The narrator seems to insist on the
young protagonist's obtuseness, revealed in the surprise attributed
to him by implication. He certainly misinterprets the morals of
Albertine, or at least her attitudes and intentions toward him, and
reflects ruefully on her virtue: "Just as we often discover a vain
miser beneath the cloak of a man famed for his bountiful charity, so
her flaunting of vice leads us to suppose a Messalina a respectable
girl with middle-class prejudices."[13] Here we see the lack of
perspicacity on his part being dissipated by the generalization (with
"we" replacing "I"); and in any case the narrator's narcissism has
little to fear from episodes which are so presented as to contrast the
younger protagonist's obtuseness with the older narrator's penetration.

The narrator accuses himself of being courageous in protecting
others not out of generosity but out of self-respect; but this confes-

sion, which gains our sympathy and no doubt our conviction as to his honesty, is followed by a passage in which every narrator's ineluctable narcissism reveals itself: "Not that this kind of unconfessed self-esteem is in any sense vanity or conceit. For what might satisfy one or other of those failings would give me no pleasure, and I have always refrained from indulging them."[14]

The difficulty of self-knowledge is of course often acknowledged by the narrator. Thus, in describing his servants' taking advantage of his weaknesses (*lacunes*), he writes: "Of these gaps I knew nothing, any more than of the salients to which they give rise, precisely because they were gaps."[15]

III   *Self-Betrayal*

Not only do defects of character which he admits lower our opinion of the narrator (except as to his accuracy or honesty); the attribution to himself of many positive qualities clearly smacks of narcissism. We may moreover judge the narrator's depth of understanding (though not his subtlety) somewhat less favorably than he himself, for while it is true that he discovers, describes, and analyzes certain psychological laws, he often does not appear to pursue them sufficiently to understand, explain, and interpret them. This is true, for example, of the laws inscribed in the bell-towers of Martinville.

Sometimes structural configurations of the work (such as repetition) provide a commentary on certain of the protagonist's actions. Our attitude to one such action is prepared by a passage in which Andrée is represented as having used a false pretext to avoid accepting his invitation; he remarks: "I ought not to have continued to seek the company of a person who was capable of uttering it. For what people have once done they will do again indefinitely, and if you go every year to see a friend who, the first time, was not able to meet you at the appointed place, or was in bed with a chill, you will find him in bed with another chill which he has just caught, you will miss him again at another meeting-place at which he has failed to appear, for a single and unalterable reason in place of which he supposes himself to have various reasons, drawn from the circumstances."[16] Just twenty pages later, we are confronted with a passage in which the protagonist is no longer the avoided but the avoider: several times, when Robert de Saint-Loup obtains a twenty-four-hour pass to go and visit him at Balbec, he puts him off on the pretext that he has to go visiting with his grandmother. This seems rather insensitive for such a hypersensitive person. Moreover, the narrator tries to counteract our condemnation (prepared by the earlier passage where he condemned Andrée) by the following comment: "No doubt I fell in his estimation when he learned from his aunt in what the 'duty call' consisted, and who the persons were who combined to play the part of my grandmother. And yet I had not been wrong, perhaps, after all, in sacrificing not only the vain pleasures of the world but the real pleasure of friendship to that of spending the whole day in this green garden. People who enjoy the capacity—it is true that such people are artists, and I had long been convinced that I should never be that—are also under an obligation to live for themselves. And friendship is a dispensation from this duty, an abdication of self."[17] This refusal to regret one's actions (an aspect, of course, of the broad theme of the passing of time) is evoked a little earlier in connection not with validated selfishness (as here) but with errors admitted and faults overcome: Bergotte declares that every mature man has said or done things he regrets and would like not to have said or done, but that such regret is an error, since his hard-won maturity or wisdom is a function of the various errors of his youth.

An overriding defect of the narrator's character is his narcissism. We have already evoked this briefly in connection with his introversion; its significance is however more general than that established by that connection. In addition to the passages already noted, there are many in which the narrator, instead of making direct complimentary statements about the protagonist, places such statements in the mouths of others. Thus he has Gilberte whisper to him: " 'You can't think how delighted I am, because you have made the conquest of my great friend Bergotte. He's been telling Mamma that he found you extremely intelligent.' "[18] He attributes to Saint-Loup a similar admiration, stating that Robert thinks himself extremely inferior to him, the protagonist. He admits that Bloch's effusions are not to be taken seriously, but quotes them nevertheless. Saint-Loup calls him (in a letter) "you fount of knowledge who have read everything" and "subtle mind and ultra-sensitive heart," referring to "all our talk . . . those hours which I never shall forget," and refers to himself as "this blunt trooper whom you will have a hard task to polish and refine, and make a little more subtle and worthier of your company."[19] Albertine says to him of her friends: "It's too good of you to attach any importance to them. You shouldn't take any notice of them; they don't count. What on earth

can a lot of kids like them mean to a man like you?"[20] Elstir tells
him "how greatly Andrée had been attracted to me"[21]—the
narrator, however, surrounds this last piece of information with a
context tinged with skepticism.

This skeptical presentation is much stronger when he reports
Bloch's compliment: " 'Believe me,' he said, 'and may the black
Ker seize me this instant and bear me across the portals of Hades,
hateful to men, if yesterday, when I thought of you, of Combray, of
my boundless affection for you, of afternoon hours in class which
you do not even remember, I did not lie awake weeping all night
long.' " The protagonist refuses to believe this compliment—but
the narrator takes the opportunity to make one to himself: "I did
not believe what he was saying, but I bore him no ill-will for that,
for I had inherited from my mother and grandmother their incapacity for resentment even of far worse offenders, and their habit
of never condemning anyone."[22]

He declares himself entirely free of vanity and pride, of which he
says: "What might satisfy one or other of those failings [vanity or
pride] would give me no pleasure, and I have always refrained from
indulging them."[23] He is also modest, and refers to "the people in
whose company I have succeeded in concealing most effectively the
slight advantages knowledge of which might have given them a less
derogatory idea of myself."[24] However, he is not incapable of seeing
through his own apparent virtues to hidden and less honorable
motives (especially when this affords him the opportunity to exhibit
his honesty and subtlety!): he remarks that his own "complete
selfishness" was modified by his grandmother's superior nature in
that he always put other people's problems before his own, but the
true reason for this is not one to be proud of: "I discovered—and
was deeply ashamed by the discovery—that it was because, in contradiction of what I had always believed and asserted, I was extremely sensitive to the opinions of others."[25] In the *Recherche*, this
sensitivity colors the tensive quality of this narrative addressed to
the reader.

Perhaps the ultimate limit in narcissism and self-flattery is
reached in the passage where he declares that his hand was sought
by the prettiest and most eligible girl in Paris, a niece of Mme. de
Guermantes, the duke being the go-between.

While the narrator derides snobbery, "a serious malady of the
spirit,"[26] the protagonist shows strong symptoms of this sickness in a
passage like the following: "The lady wore an air of extreme dig-

nity; and as I, for my part, bore within me the consciousness that I
was invited, two days later, to the terminal point of the little
railway, by the famous Mme Verdurin, that at an intermediate sta-
tion I was awaited by Robert de Saint-Loup, and that a little farther
on I had it in my power to give great pleasure to Mme de Cambremer, by going to stay at Féterne, my eyes sparkled with irony as
I studied this self-important lady who seemed to think that, because
of her elaborate attire, the feathers in her hat, her *Revue des Deux
Mondes*, she was a more considerable personage than myself."[27]
The narrator's snobbery is evident in the irony directed against M.
Verdurin: " 'I attach no importance whatever to titles of nobility,'
he went on, with that contemptuous smile which I have seen so
many people whom I have known, unlike my grandmother and my
mother, assume when they spoke of anything that they did not
possess, before others who thus, they supposed, would be prevented
from using that particular advantage to crow over them."[28] It is obvious, if somewhat tempered by sympathy, in the following passage
on Albertine: "She had assumed, on hearing the proud title and
great name, that air more than indifferent, hostile, contemptuous,
which is the sign of an impotent desire in proud and passionate
natures."[29]

At times, he attempts to gain our sympathy by affecting a certain
modesty: "Who can say whether, seen from without, some man of
talent, or even a man devoid of talent, but a lover of the things of
the mind, myself for instance, would not have appeared, to anyone
who met him at Rivebelle, at the hotel at Balbec, or on the beach
there, the most perfect and pretentious imbecile?"[30] He admits that
Albertine gave up the idea of marrying him, as he says, "because of
my indecisive and cantankerous character."[31]

Masochism seems to be a basic tendency of the protagonist's personality: "I was falling ever faster and faster down the slope of my
wretchedness, towards an ever more profound despair, and with the
inertia of a man who feels the cold grip him, makes no effort to
resist it and even finds a sort of pleasure in shivering."[32] The
narrator eventually, in the last volume, develops this into a full-
blown philosophy of literary creation, equating happiness with the
sleep of the mind and exalting the positive value of suffering to our
efforts to understand the human condition. The traditional conflict
between mind (spirit, soul) and body, postulated by Christianity but
rejected by Zola and others, is reinstated by the narrator of the
Recherche: "Happiness is beneficial for the body but it is grief that

develops the powers of the mind."[33] Giving the preference to the mind, alone productive of art, the narrator necessarily rejects happiness, which he sees as nothing more than a useful foil to set off unhappiness and make it more vivid. Suffering is exalted for its role as catalyst: "Imagination and reflection may be admirable machines in themselves but they may stand idle unless suffering furnishes the motive power."[34] The narrator does have a moment's hesitation as to the general validity of this perspective (but he quickly suppresses it): "Perhaps only in a few great geniuses does this upsurging constantly go on without their having need to be stirred by suffering; and yet, perhaps, when we study the abundant and regular development of their joyous work, we are too much inclined to infer that their lives were joyful also, whereas, on the contrary, they may have been continually filled with sorrow."[35]

Cowardice is another personal characteristic of the protagonist (deriving from his symbiotic relationship with others, his hypersensitivity, and his passivity) which he turns into a general tendency of all men: "In my cowardice I became at once a man, and did what all we grown men do when face to face with suffering and injustice; I preferred not to see them."[36] He speaks also of his "want of self-importance and resentment": "Anger and spite came to me only in a wholly different manner, in furious crises. What was more, the sense of justice was so far lacking in me as to amount to an entire want of moral sense."[37]

Another feature of the protagonist's manner of relating to others is his selfishness. It is evident in individual actions or projects, such as the manner in which he plans to break with Albertine, waiting until she has gone out, then getting ready and going off himself, to Venice, leaving her a message but not seeing her again. It also emerges from more general habits of conduct: he blames Albertine severely for her interest in other young men or women, although he considers his own similar interest quite blameless. Again, he generalizes to include everybody in this pattern of conduct: "We [on] consider it innocent to desire a thing and atrocious that the other person should desire it."[38] And he has M. de Charlus act exactly the same way with Morel as the protagonist does with Albertine.

As for his tendency to lie and cheat: "Untruthfulness and dishonesty were with me, as with most people, called into being in so immediate, so contingent a fashion . . . that my mind, fixed on some lofty ideal, allowed my character, in the darkness below, to set about those urgent, sordid tasks, and did not look down to observe them."[39]

IV *Surrogate Selves*

Let us recall the "ridiculous or hateful incarnations" mentioned by Bergotte. Each of these previous incarnations, however regrettable and rejected by the present Self, represents a sort of alter ego: there is identification (here, through physical continuity—as between protagonist and narrator when we look forward instead of backward), but it is only partial. The degree of resemblance must remain a moot point. There is, however, another kind of alter ego in the work, represented by an actual separate character.

Within the protagonist's family there are strong resemblances between himself and others, and Tante Léonie is a veritable alter ego: "Among the sensual expressions, we may recognize others that were peculiar to my grandmother and mother for, little by little, I was beginning to resemble all my relatives, my father who—in a very different fashion from myself, no doubt, for if things do repeat themselves, it is with great variations—took so keen an interest in the weather; and not my father only, I was becoming more and more like my aunt Léonie."[40] He dwells on this particular resemblance at some length: "It was quite enough that I should bear an exaggerated resemblance to my father, to the extent of not being satisfied like him with consulting the barometer, but becoming an animated barometer myself; it was quite enough that I should allow myself to be ordered by my aunt Léonie to stay at home and watch the weather from my bedroom window or even from my bed; yet here I was talking now to Albertine, at one moment as the child that I had been at Combray used to talk to my mother, at another as my grandmother used to talk to me."[41]

Another such alter ego for the narrator is Andrée, whose resemblance to the young protagonist is expressly indicated: "For me really to love Andrée, she was too intellectual, too neurotic, too sickly, too much like myself. If Albertine now seemed to me to be void of substance, Andrée was filled with something which I knew only too well."[42] Indeed, Andrée unconsciously imitates the protagonist's manner of speaking, resembles him in her narcissism, and even looks like him without his moustache. The narrator exploits this identification for narcissistic ends, through compliments paid to the protagonist through Andrée: "She expressed her

friendship for me, for Albertine, in terms which were evidence of
the most exquisite understanding of the things of the heart, which
may have been partly due to the state of her health."[43] This identification also throws an interesting light on the relationship
between Andrée and Albertine: "Admiration and attention had so
heated Albertine that great drops were rolling down her cheeks. Andrée preserved the unruffled calm of a female dandy."[44] The role of
intellectual (but not physical) dominance given here to the alter ego
Andrée in her relationship with Albertine will be accompanied by
suggestions of physical relations, and prefigures that to be played
later by the protagonist himself.

We have already noted the identification of the protagonist with
M. de Charlus. This character, whose homosexuality is given the
name of "Charlism," is related by his name to Charles (Swann) and
Charlie (Morel), each of whom provides a further alter ego for the
protagonist. The less important by far is Morel, who represents essentially two traits of the protagonist: first, he is the sort of good-
looking young man who attracts a pederast like M. de Charlus; and
second, he is obsessively attracted to the deflowering of virgins.
Each of these potentialities of the protagonist's character is
developed at length in the career of Morel. The second may not
seem appropriate to the protagonist's passive, compassionate
nature, but it is suggested by a passage like the following: "We
know no rest until we can discover by experiment whether the
proud girl on the seashore, the shop-assistant on her high horse of
'What will people say?,' the pre-occupied fruit seller cannot be
made, by skilful handling on our part, to relax their rectangular attitude, to throw about our neck their fruit-laden arms, to direct
towards our lips, with a smile of consent, eyes hitherto frozen or
absent."[45]

The most important alter ego (always a solution to the problem of
escaping from the self) is Charles Swann. The protagonist imagined
that Swann would have laughed at his anguish at being separated
from the loved one, but later realizes that in fact Swann was
supremely qualified to appreciate this particular kind of suffering.
The protagonist resembles Swann in many traits, some of which are
implicit and left for the reader to perceive (taste for young girls),
while others are explicitly indicated: the taste for women as incarnations of a certain type, class, or place; the tendency to be a "lover
of phantoms";[46] the capacity to play a role in society as a "man of
fine position although not titled."[47] Swann, like the protagonist,

prefers in women a beauty "as fresh and plump as a rose."[48] The chief resemblances, however, concern the relations between the protagonist and Albertine on the one hand and between Swann and Odette on the other—resemblances which are sometimes the result not of mere coincidence but of actual influence.

The *Recherche* shows the self slowly awakening, from light sleep or deep slumber, sometimes from dreams or half-dreams, to a sense of existence, however fragmentary. Gradually the narrator develops a self-portrait: the protagonist is sickly, emotional, and neurotic; he is generally sensitive and intelligent, but sometimes naive and even obtuse. Various faults emerge *as if* by accident: narcissism, snobbery, masochism, cowardice, selfishness, dishonesty. A favorite means of fleshing out this self-portrait is the depiction of surrogate selves such as Aunt Léonie, Andrée, M. de Charlus, Morel, and especially Swann.

CHAPTER 3

Relationships

I *Parthenogenesis and Egocentrism*

IN the *Recherche* we find ourselves progressively spiraling outward from the self: after sketching its own diversification and its identification with others, the narrating consciousness depicts its alienation from self and its submersion in the other. Thus we move from a relatively active and affirmative view of others as selves to a relatively passive and vulnerable view of self as other.

From the opening pages we are confronted with the theme of self and a striking thesis concerning it, namely, that it is the self which makes (or projects) the world which it then thinks it "comes to know." The narrator is led to evoke the generation of imaginary others (in this case, a woman) through a working of the imagination stimulated by sense-impressions. Shortly thereafter, this theme of the imaginative construction of a subjective "reality" will recur in the form of a variation, dealing with the fabrication of false images of the other through the hasty, overzealous, and insufficiently flexible activity of the intellect. This activity produces oversimplified conceptions of various acquaintances of the protagonist and his family. An early and extreme example is that of Swann, whom the family is convinced it knows: as a result, any evidence that Swann is actually different from this firm conviction (any evidence, for instance, of his leading a brilliant social life inaccessible to them) is dismissed as misleading. Other examples are provided by Legrandin and Cottard. Subtle but dramatic changes in facial expression are brilliantly described: Legrandin, M. de Norpois, Andrée, Françoise; but of course observation (and even evocation, description) does not necessarily prove penetration.

The notion that the self creates the world around it (at least in some sense) occurs several times in the *Recherche*. The narrator

43

refers, for example, to "the age in which one believes that one gives a thing real existence by giving it a name,"[1] and repeatedly stresses the subjectivity of our perception of others: "We never see the people who are dear to us save in the animated system, the perpetual motion of our incessant love for them, which before allowing the images that their faces present to reach us catches them in its vortex, flings them back upon the idea we have always had of them, makes them adhere to it, coincide with it."[2] Existence *as perceptible,* that is, presence, is dependent on consciousness: "It is our noticing them that puts things in a room, our growing used to them that takes them away again and clears a space for us."[3] This theme is developed further in a reference to "my eyes—which the things in my room in Paris disturbed me no more than did my eyelids themselves, for they were merely extensions of my organs, an enlargement of myself."[4] Presence is thus identified with consciousness, and just as the presence of other things and other people is dependent on our consciousness of them, so also our presence depends on the consciousness of others: "I was in the room, or rather I was not yet in the room since she was not aware of my presence. . . . One enjoys during the brief moment of return the faculty of being a spectator, so to speak, of one's own absence."[5]

This principle of subjective perception, frequently taken as far as actual imaginative creation, is applied, like so many other principles in the *Recherche,* to the relationship most closely and fully studied throughout the work, namely, love, which is presented as a prime example of parthenogenesis; we fall in love not with a particular person but with an idea which we project upon a person: "My love was not so much a love for her as a love in myself."[6] The narrator writes of the women we love that they are a product of our temperament, an image, an inverted projection, a "negative" of our sensibility. He affirms repeatedly (with Stendhal) that love is subjective and founded on a desire which preexists the object (reduced thus to a mere pretext): it is the lover's passion that creates the beloved.

The illusory nature of desire is demonstrated by the fact that it self-destructs if excessive (the pretext is rendered inadequate by a preexistent ideal), while it is stimulated by frustration. The love of Swann for Odette illustrates this point at length. General laws are extracted from the protagonist's experiences and the narrator's observations. Love is a mistake: "a sentiment which (whatever its cause) is invariably in error."[7] Love is a sickness ("the general sickness called love")[8] and serves to illustrate "the disastrous manner in which the psychopathic universe is constructed."[9] The strain between the protagonist's individual experience and the narrator's desire to draw general laws from it sometimes shows: "In a love which is not reciprocated—I might as well say, in love, for there are people for whom there is no such thing as reciprocated love—. . . ."[10] Such statements reflect the narrator's introversion, which we have already discussed, as does the following: "We wish to be understood, because we wish to be loved, and we wish to be loved because we are in love. The understanding of other people is immaterial and their love importunate."[11] The narrator clearly tends to give a general validity to his own experience and observations: "It is the lot of a certain period in life which may come to us quite early that we are made less amorous by a person than by a desertion."[12] Insofar as the form of this statement gives it generality, it remains badly in need of further substantiation. On the other hand, in so far as its content ("a certain period in life") restricts its application, it is more acceptable. It does appear, indeed, that the type of love described by the narrator is essentially and irremediably immature, as revealed by passages affirming the absolute necessity of pretending indifference. Such a conception of love is essentially introverted, selfish, alienating, linked to the notion of possession (rather than to that of a shared and generous relationship)—in spite of the admission at another point that in the act of possession one really possesses nothing at all.

For other reasons also we must ask whether the laws of love arrived at by the narrator do possess the general validity he tends to give them. While one easily accepts that sadistic and masochistic impulses are often associated with certain forms of love, the absolutely central function attributed to them here is debatable. The protagonist is not only unkind to Albertine, he admits that he *enjoys* making her suffer. His persecution of her seems to him so basic and natural for someone in love that the narrator arrives at the following generalization: "To be harsh and deceitful to the person whom we love is so natural! . . . A stranger leaves us indifferent, and indifference does not prompt us to unkind actions."[13] Thus love is seen as always and inevitably sadistic—a conclusion of dubious validity.

Love is also masochistic: "Desire, going always in the direction of what is most opposite to ourself, forces us to love what will make us suffer."[14] In fact, attraction to another person is a product of our unconscious realization that such a person is capable of making us

suffer. An interesting manifestation of masochism is the narrator's
guilt complex: because he fell out of love with Albertine and failed
to show enough compassion toward his dying grandmother, he
blames himself for their deaths and for inflicting another death on
them by his forgetfulness. He prays to expiate his crimes by illness
and pain. His guilt complex is based partly on the fact that his
grandfather's and great-aunt's treatment of his grandmother, which
is his archetype of cruelty, and his own treatment of her are
associated in his mind. Again, however, we find the urge to
generalize: pain is presented as one of the chief modes of
relationship between self and other, so that it is only natural for the
lesbianism of Mlle. Vinteuil to involve elements of exhibitionism
and of sadism. Sadism and masochism are in fact intimately related
to our learning and maturing, which takes us through pain to
knowledge.

II *Classification*

Certain social relationships reflect depersonalization, dehumanization, and alienation. One example is provided by the absolute code of conduct observed by Françoise: "For things which
might or might not be done, she possessed a code at once imperious,
abundant, subtle, and uncompromising on points themselves im-
perceptible or irrelevant."[15]

Such coded and indeed petrified modes of behavior are also to be
found later—in the young protagonist's rating-scale of actors and
actresses, in his family's manner of judging the life of his uncle
Adolphe, and so on. Such, for example, is the relationship between
real people and mere categories like that of the scullery maid:
Françoise had a different one to help her every year, but the position constituted a permanent institution, a sort of moral personality
or character, with unvarying characteristics and responsibilities.
Prostitutes are similarly indistinguishable from one another:
"[They] are of no interest because they remain invariable."[16] The
Duchesse de Guermantes is in a somewhat similar situation, more a
category than a real person, so that when the real person appears,
the idea of what the category (the title, in this case) entails soon
drives out any elements which may conflict with the preconceived
idea.

Another way in which the self relates to the other is through nam-
ing. The notion that the secret essence of the person is somehow im-

prisoned in his or her name, so that to know the name is to seize and penetrate the very person of the being to whom it belongs (or who belongs to it), is current among primitive tribes, as Claude Lévi-Strauss relates. Our protagonist has such a view of names, as we first perceive from his reaction to such names as Champi, Gilberte, Swann, Perchamps, or even a mere syllable like *-antes*. It would appear to relate both to Adamic language, in which there was identity between an object and its name, and to children's belief in such an identity, as studied by Jean Piaget.

This tendency to classify people into a hierarchy or a typology, whether he is dealing with actors or with officers, is basic to the protagonist's character. The reduction of several individuals to variations on one stereotype (the actor, the officer), which he also carries out (and much more readily) with respect to the various women loved by one man, has its counterpart in the splintering of one individual into many different versions—various Odettes, various Albertines: as he remarks, "in the infinite series of imaginary Albertines who followed one after the other in my fancy, hour after hour, the real Albertine, a glimpse caught on the beach, figured only at the head, just as the actress who creates a part, the star, appears, out of a long series of performances, in the few first alone."[17] This process is facilitated by doubts as to the reality of other people or at least of our image of them: a woman encountered in a little Gothic street is taken by him as a pure emanation of the Middle Ages. This is why love and friendship strike him as illusions: they put us in contact not with others but with images projected by our own emotions: "Is not the indication of the unreality of the others sufficiently evident either in their inability to satisfy us, . . . or in the despondency that follows whatever satisfaction they may give?"[18] The spectacle of dramatic characters dissolving at the end of a play leads him to "doubt the reality of our ego and meditate on the mystery of death."[19]

The unsubstantiality of others is further suggested by the importance attached (and this goes beyond Stendhal's theory of the subjectivity of love) to the role of obstacles and absence in the development of desire: attraction to a person is one thing, but love, with all its anguish, sorrow, and suggestion of the irrevocable, cannot establish itself without some appearance of insuperable barriers standing in the way. He gives examples from his own experience: when he feels absolutely confident of a future pleasure, his enjoyment of the thought of it diminishes; when his confidence is shaken, the at-

traction of the prospect returns in full force. As usual, he develops a
general law from his own limited observations: "Variance of a belief, annulment also of love, which, preexistent and mobile, comes
to rest at the image of any one woman simply because that woman
will be almost impossible of attainment."[20] It is true that he does
allege another example provided by Saint-Loup's relationship with
Rachel: "As soon as he realized that a definite rupture has been
avoided, he saw all the disadvantages of a reconciliation."[21]

A fundamental theme is that of the preference for solitude, which
is not only necessary even for the tasting of aesthetic pleasures but
absolutely essential for artists, who wish to create and should not
allow themselves to be distracted by time-wasting illusions like
social intercourse and friendship. An exception is made for love, but
only because it causes sufferings that stimulate the artist.

III *Symbiosis*

From the very first pages of the work we find the protagonist
deeply immersed in a relationship with the mother, a relationship so
powerful and all-absorbing that his very existence is threatened by
it: death by falling from a window is not considered too high a price
to pay for one good-night kiss.

The price of this kiss will be paid initially by the mother: "It
struck me that if I had just scored a victory it was over her; that I
had succeeded, as sickness or sorrow or age might have succeeded,
in relaxing her will, in altering her judgment; that this evening
opened a new era, must remain a black date in the calendar. . . . I
felt that I had with an impious and secret finger traced a first
wrinkle upon her soul and made the first white hair show upon her
head."[22] We are not told *why* the mother must thus pay the price of
the kiss by age and mortality. Perhaps the answer is that time has
weakened the parents' capacity to keep refusing the demands of the
child's excessive sensibility, and this weakening effect of time is
demonstrated for the first time by this first acquiescence. Until this
point, the mother's admiration of (and submission to) the father had
kept the child in the position of "excluded third" in the triangle;[23]
now, however, the father's change of attitude encourages the
development of the mother-child symbiosis, which will effectively
transfer the "undifferentiation" detectable in the parent couple
from the latter to the child.[24]

As a result, a heavy price will also be paid by the son: he will refer to his victory as "what was, perhaps, the sweetest and the saddest night of my life (when I had, alas . . . obtained from my parents the initial abdication, from which I can date the decline in my health and my will power and the daily increasing habit of postponing a difficult task)."[25] The reason, of course, is that on that day the parents renounced the struggle to force the child to differentiate a self by foregoing the fusion with the mother to which he had become addicted. This has the effect of limiting his ability to attain a reasonable level of (basic) self, necessary for autonomous goal-oriented activity. Separation from his mother becomes a catastrophe, as when he leaves to holiday at Balbec with his grandmother: "For the first time I began to feel that it was possible that my mother might live without me, otherwise than for me, a separate life."[26]

The older narrator's ultimate achievement in writing his lengthy autobiography reflects the final dissolution of the various bonds which had inhibited his differentiation of a self; but while the actual act of literary creation is for him an act of liberation, the nature of the work produced reflects continuing traces of undifferentiation.

The protagonist has a symbiotic relationship not only with his mother but also with his grandmother, who is presented as a profoundly meaningful surrogate for the mother. He declares his mother and his grandmother "my models in all things,"[27] and finds in his grandmother "a desire to save and prolong my life stronger than was my own; and my thoughts were continued in her without having to undergo any deflection, since they passed from my mind into hers without change of atmosphere or of personality."[28] The grandmother unites an extreme desire for the natural (walks in the rain and the wind) with an equally extreme desire for the artificial (prefers sketches to photographs). (This apparent contradiction may be explained by the fact that both types of experience represent examples of symbiosis—she becomes one with the wind and the rain; and the scene is blended with an artist's particular reaction, vision, and personality.) He declares that his grandmother has as close a relationship with his mother as Mme. de Sévigné with *her* daughter, and he emphasizes the influence of parents on their children. His mother eventually gives up trying to break his symbiosis with her: "Nowadays she was well aware that an apparent coldness on her part would alter nothing, and the affection that she lavished upon me was like those forbidden foods which are no longer withheld from invalids when it is certain that they are past recovery."[29] He does make some attempts at autonomy, but these are desperate, painful, and unsuccessful.[30] The protagonist's fundamental unwillingness to forego the pleasures of symbiosis are perhaps best summed up in the following passage: "How I suffered from that position to which we are reduced by the carelessness of nature which, when instituting the division of bodies, never thought of making possible the interpenetration of souls."[31]

Besides the parent-child symbiosis, other relationships militate against the differentiation of self. The family, for instance, may constitute an ego mass which is inimical to differentiation and autonomy. Such is the family situation of the Proustian protagonist. This undifferentiated family ego mass is clearly demonstrated by the attitude of condescension toward outsiders, illustrated, for example, by the family's amusement at their ignorance of family customs, such as that of lunching an hour earlier on Saturdays:

The surprise of a "barbarian" (for so we termed everyone who was not acquainted with Saturday's special customs) who had called at eleven o'clock to speak to my father, and had found us at table, was an event which used to cause Françoise as much merriment as, perhaps, anything that had ever happened in her life. And if she found it amusing that the nonplussed visitor should not have know, beforehand, that we had our luncheon an hour earlier on Saturdays, it was still more irresistibly funny that my father himself (fully as she sympathized, from the bottom of her heart, with the rigid chauvinism which prompted him) should never have dreamed that the barbarian could fail to be aware of so simple a matter, and so had replied, with no further enlightenment of the other's surprise at seeing us already in the diningroom: "You see, it's Saturday."[32]

Indeed, one of the chief functions of the character Françoise is to illustrate this feeling for family and to distinguish it from other kinds of relationship. It is true that she remains irreducibly individual in her attitudes to her own emotions and those of her family, and the "the unwritten laws of her time-honoured Code" guarantee her a certain autonomy in her relations with them;[33] but the same Code, which she imagines gives her certain rights and privileges,[34] dictates a fine sense of what is due to them: "She was one of those Combray servants, conscious of their master's place in the world, and that the least that they can do is to see that he is treated with all the respect to which they consider him entitled."[35] Her symbiotic relationship with the family is profound and explicit: "Françoise's relationship with us was symbiotic; it was we who, with our virtues, our wealth, our style of living, must take on ourselves the task of concocting those little sops to her vanity out of which was formed . . . the portion of happiness indispensable to her existence."[36]

It may appear at times that Françoise is capable of altruistic concern for others, as in her weeping and sobbing when she reads about the suffering caused (to imaginary—or, at best, putative—others) by imprisonment or illness; however, this is not genuine altruism but pseudoaltruism, as we see from the vast difference between her attitudes to such vague, unknown others and to the true others we may term "outsiders," in binary opposition to "insiders." This distinction is made as follows: "Françoise, who, for her own daughter or for her nephews, would have given her life without a murmur, showed a singular implacability in her dealings with the rest of the world."[37] Her devotion to her grandson contrasts violently with her cruelty toward the scullery maid. The difference between "outsider" and "pseudo-outsider" is illustrated by the following passage: "Apart from her own kinsfolk, the sufferings of humanity inspired in her a pity which increased in direct ratio to the distance separating the sufferers from herself. The tears which flowed from her in torrents when she read of the misfortunes of persons unknown to her, in a newspaper, were quickly stemmed once she had been able to form a more accurate mental picture of the victims."[38] Through the falsity of her sympathy for vague and unreal others ("that pleasant sensation of tenderness and pity"),[39] and through her distinction between "outsiders" and "insiders," Françoise applies the values of (and symbolically represents) the undifferentiated family ego mass with its incapacity for genuine altruistic concern for others.[40] This role of hers is emphasized by her "insider" conception of her master's family, especially as reflected in her grief at the death of Aunt Léonie, which leaves her "inspired like a poet with a flood of confused reflections upon bereavement, grief, and family memories"[41]—for, as she remarks of the rather dotty old lady, "she did belong, all the same, to your *geology*."

The emotional fusion among its members and differentiation from others typical of the undifferentiated family ego mass is characteristic of any such social group. A prime example is provided by the *clan Verdurin*, which the narrator evokes thus: "Each 'new recruit' whom the Verdurins failed to persuade that the evenings spent by other people, in other houses than theirs, were as dull as ditch-water, saw himself banished forthwith."[42] Autonomy of a member poses a threat and cannot be tolerated, and coherence is maintained through exclusion, which masquerades as exclusivity: external differentiation guarantees internal "undifferentiation."[43] "Just as the 'good pals' came to take a more and more prominent place in Mme Verdurin's life, so the 'bores,' the 'nuisances' grew to include everybody and everything that kept her friends away from her, that made them sometimes plead 'previous engagements': the mother of one, the professional duties of another, the 'little place in the country' of a third."[44] There is thus a movement toward a fusion within the group so complete that hostility is attributed not only to competing *salons* and *soirées* but to all outside factors—and once the whole environment is perceived as hostile, the door is open to total emotional and mental imbalance. The level of self within such a group is obviously at its lowest ebb.[45]

An individual sentimental relationship poses its own special threat to the group.

If one of the "faithful" had a friend, or one of the ladies a young man, who was liable, now and then, to make them miss an evening, the Verdurins, who were not in the least afraid of a woman's having a lover, provided that she had him in their company, loved him in their company, and did not prefer him to their company, would say: "Very well, then, bring your friend along." And he would be put to the test, to see whether he was willing to have no secrets from Mme Verdurin, whether he was susceptible of being enrolled in the "little clan." If he failed to pass, the faithful one who had introduced him would be taken on one side, and would be tactfully assisted to quarrel with the friend or mistress.[46]

The principle applied is not "If you can't beat them, join them" but in a sense the reverse: "If you can't get them to join you by absorption: that is, by abandonment of self-differentiation, then destroy them by exclusion and by using gossip or some such means to destroy the threatening relationship with the clan member."[47]

In the case of the *salon Verdurin*, the narrator attributes the experience not to himself when young but to Swann. It is clear, however, from many circumstances, as we have shown elsewhere, that Swann is the protagonist's alter ego, and through Swann the narrator conveys to us *from the inside* an extreme experience of having to sacrifice one's basic self, differentiation, and individual autonomy as a propitiatory offering, to be devoured by the group's insatiable demands for fusion and undifferentiation.

IV *Schizophrenia*

Modern family behavior theory has established that difficulties in achieving psychological and emotional autonomy are often caused by excessive symbiosis with parents, family, or other groups, a situation commonly productive of schizophrenia. Now, many elements of the *Recherche*, as we have just seen, appear to reflect such symbiosis, and their analysis in terms of schizophrenia may therefore offer the possibility of developing a new interpretation of the *Recherche*.

This interpretation is supported by (and provides a key to) other aspects of the Proustian universe which I shall deal with later; at this point I shall limit myself to arguing the case for schizophrenia as related to symbiosis. Not that Proust himself is necessarily schizophrenic, of course—the widespread practice of drawing conclusions about an author from a study of his work is of dubious validity, and this is particularly true of the practice of confusing an author with his first-person narrator; my thesis is rather that Proust has, whether intentionally or not, executed a brilliant portrayal of a schizophrenic narrator, or at least a schizophrenic protagonist.

In a noted theoretical work, Gilles Deleuze and Felix Guattari accuse Proust of schizophrenia.[48] Here schizophrenia is located not on the level of the Freudian family but on two other levels, the one below and the other above, namely, the microcosmic and the macrocosmic (or what they term the "molecular" and the "molar") levels, the family being merely an agent for the displacement of these more authentic but repressed pressures. On the "molar" level the hypothesis developed is that, in the modern political state, the castrating father-figure of the Freudian Oedipus complex is replaced by the state itself (the *archi-Etat*, or *Urstaat*). The Marxist notion of a historical dialectic, the next phase of which will see the capitalist system reach its limits and self-destruct, is replaced by a perspective in which capitalism may progress indefinitely from one insane crisis to another, ever more severe and alienating; the dialectic is replaced by growing schizophrenia. In the *Recherche*, says Deleuze, the "molar" level is illustrated by the protagonist's inability to distinguish Albertine from the rest of the group of young girls. The "molecular" level, on the other hand, is evidenced by his being no longer able, in proximity, to grasp Albertine (or even Albertine's face) as a whole. Deleuze says of the scene where the narrator kisses

Albertine:[49] "At last, in close proximity, everything falls apart like a vision on the sand, Albertine's face breaks up into partial, molecular objects, while the parts of the narrator's face approximate a body without organs, eyes closed, nose blocked, mouth full."[50] The "partial objects" and the "bodies without organs" are classical symptoms of their "molecular" schizophrenia.

According to another hypothesis, developed not by a Proust critic but by a specialist in schizophrenia,[51] one characteristic of this illness is that schizophrenics live in a world of blinding light, a condition which is treated by the use of dark colors. It is possible to apply this conception to the *Recherche:* the protagonist is torn between desire for the bright sunshine, *which he associates however with his malady,* and need for the darker hues associated with rainy weather. He evokes a "little person inside me, hymning the rising sun,"[52] and declares: "I may be suffering from a choking fit which the mere threat of rain would calm; he pays no heed, and at the first drops so impatiently awaited, losing his gaiety, sullenly pulls down his hood."[53] This passion for bright sunshine is accompanied by an obsession with the Guermantes, who, through their golden hair, are embodiments of the sun—a symbolic function mentioned explicitly several times in the text.

The perspective proposed here, while arguing for schizophrenia in the *Recherche,* is based on a totally different conception of schizophrenia and a radically different analysis of the *Recherche.* It is based on clinical research into family interrelationships, which has shown that an excessively symbiotic relationship between mother and child produces schizophrenia in the latter:[54] the greater the degree of emotional fusion with the mother, the lower the degree of self-differentiation, and the greater the difficulty for the child to "differentiate a self"[55]—that is, to achieve healthy autonomy, whether emotional, psychological, or mental. The level of basic self (autonomous position stances, not negotiable in the relationship system) remains low, while the pseudoself, acquired through the relationship and negotiable within it, tends to dominate. This pseudoself trades beliefs and principles in order to enhance its position within the relationship and thus earn love and security, and it is this pseudoself which fuses with others in an intense emotional field.[56]

People whose level of basic self is low "have no choice but continued pursuit of a close relationship for gratification of emotional 'needs.'"[57] Fusion may take place not only with one other person (for example, the mother) but also with a group of people—typically, the family. Through such emotional fusion, great pressure may be exerted upon the self to abandon (or at least suspend) objectivity and accept the values and attitudes of what has been termed the "undifferentiated family ego mass."[58] Both types of fusion are detectable in *A la recherche du temps perdu*, and strongly suggest a low level of self in the protagonist; and this conception of schizophrenia may be both more valid in itself and more effective a key to the Proustian universe than that offered by Deleuze.

My thesis as to these various groups' role in inhibiting the narrator's differentiation of a self is confirmed by the fact that it is only when they have dissolved that he achieves the autonomy necessary for the writing of his great work. (Even then, as I have already mentioned, the work itself is marked by certain traces of continuing undifferentiation.)

Both these and other aspects of the Proustian narration appear to be best explained by use of the particular conception of schizophrenia derived from recent clinical research into family behavior and psychotherapy.

As the Self reaches out from its narrow cocoon, it first encounters its own projections rather than really external reality, for our conceptions are subjective and what we are unconscious of does not exist for us. Love is not inspired by the beloved but projected upon her; it is an error and a sickness, inherently sadistic and masochistic, and since it is largely dependent on frustration it cannot be shared. Such egocentric views as these (all highly debatable, at least in part) relate the narrator's conception of love to his general view of others as unreal and illusory—mere illustrations of impersonal categories of being, whether personal (as in one's various mistresses), social, or geographical. Insofar as the protagonist *does* make contact with another real being, it is with his mother; and this relationship is all-absorbing and therefore destructive—so symbiotic as to inhibit the achievement of emotional and psychological autonomy. This inhibiting symbiosis is represented (in fact, imposed) on the social level by the family and by the *clan Verdurin*. The result of such symbiosis, as modern family behavior theory has established, is schizophrenia in the form of lack of self-differentiation.

CHAPTER 4

People

I   *The Alienation of Social Discourse*

A S we spiral out beyond not only the self but also the self-other relationship, we encounter the broad level of society—a multitude of others not only prepared to relate to the protagonist but further possessed of their own interrelationships, many of which constitute veritable codes of belief, of evaluation, and of conduct. Social intercourse requires that the self submit itself to the process of learning these codes and of adopting them, a process as alienating (from the immediate experience of phenomena) as is the earlier absorption of one's mother tongue, with its ready-made concepts, categories, and organization.

The self cannot, however, evade the necessity of this initiation, for its self-concept or self-image requires confirmation from society's acceptance, with all the constraints this acceptance involves. Just how far an individual may be driven to go in this need to establish a favorable self-image is reflected in the portraits of Albertine and M. de Norpois, who employ what the narrator terms *le système des fins multiples* ("multiple-goal system"): this consists in trying to persuade several people that one particular action was done solely for the sake of each of them. Thus Albertine attributes her actions (for example, a visit) to the motivation most flattering to the person she is addressing. This type of falsehood, which the narrator attributes to Albertine's desire to give pleasure, is really much less altruistic: it is essentially narcissistic, her aim being above all to make others think well of her. This is clearly revealed in the keen reaction experienced by the protagonist (now mere surprise, now acute embarrassment) at discovering the lively impressions he had unwittingly made on people in the past. Again, the characters involved are Albertine and M. de Norpois. He discovers that Albertine recalls in extraordinary detail his own actions on the day they first met; this particular remembrance is of course rather flattering. That involving M. de Norpois is not, for the diplomat makes an embarrassing allusion to an evening years ago when he was convinced the protagonist was on the point of kissing his hands from gratitude.

A striking feature of the interpersonal relationships portrayed in the *Recherche* is their inauthenticity, caused primarily by the role played by money. (There are of course other causes, such as selfishness, unbridled sexual passion, and so on.) This inauthenticity affects relationships both heterosexual (for example, Swann/Odette, the narrator/Albertine) and homosexual (for example, Charlus/Morel), and it contributes to a distorted view of love on the part of the narrator, thus diminishing the validity of his conclusions and generalizations. No doubt Odette and Albertine may have genuine feelings for Swann and the protagonist respectively, but these feelings are vitiated by economic pressures and by the man's suspicions regarding their foundation. In other words, the self-other relationship is interfered with and corrupted by a third element coming from beyond the couple—from a social structure based on financial disparities.[1]

Odette is a "kept woman": in payment for his visits, she accepts cash gifts at the end of the month from Swann; she does not hesitate to ask him for money to pay her debts or rent a chateau for the Wagner season; and Swann is convinced that his fortune alone prevents her from breaking with him. What is particularly striking (and odious) is the fact that Swann is quite happy about this corrupt relationship.

Albertine also is a "kept woman": indeed, the protagonist's tempting of her with the hope of a wealthy marriage, a car, a yacht, and so on is disgusting, and it is scarcely any wonder that she sighs "Ah! if only I had an income of three hundred thousand francs . . . "[2]—a moment of weakness and truth that she is immediately forced to cover up with another of her many lies. The narrator calls this "a nasty avowal," but what is "nasty" is his crude purchasing of her body and even, to some extent, her mind. Rare are the moments when he faces his moral responsibility: "Since I had continued to spend so much money upon her, I had taken her notwithstanding this moral baseness; this baseness I had maintained in her, I had perhaps increased, perhaps created it."[3] Too often he rejoices at these financial and social advantages, even while trying to depreciate their effectiveness: "Albertine had been penniless, obscure, she must have been anxious to marry me. And yet I had not been able to possess her exclusively. Whatever be our social position, however wise our precautions, when the truth is confessed we have no hold over the life of another person."[4] Nothing could be more false than this conclusion: everything suggests, on the contrary, that Albertine was attracted to him largely because of his money and left him because of his suspicions and persecution and to satisfy an unfulfilled sexual appetite.

It is all the more absurd for Marxist critics like Georgy Lukács to neglect modern writers like Proust in that they provide brilliant support and illustration of the thesis as to the advanced stage of alienation detectable in the capitalist society of the Belle Epoque, where dehumanization was rampant in the form of the purchasing power of money as applied even to human beings. Several different causes of social decay and change (through mingling of the classes) are studied, from the political (the Dreyfus case) to the sexual (for example, Swann's heterosexuality, Charlus' homosexuality), but no cause is more dramatically portrayed than the alienating role of money and the immensity of its arbitrary power, reflected in the ruin of the Prince de Guermantes and his subsequent (and consequent) marriage with Mme. Verdurin.

While the depiction and interpretation of the penetration of certain members of the bourgeoisie, and even of the working class, into the ranks of the aristocracy is convincing,[5] the narrator shows, in his study of individual cases, a deplorable inability to believe in the existence of mutual, unselfish, and profound relationships between equals—apparently because his own pathologically abnormal manner of relating to others has prevented him from experiencing such a relationship (or of recognizing it for what it was if he did experience it).

Social alienation is further reflected in the fact that others see not our mind and heart (our "soul") but our body—as we theirs. Many are the physical portraits of various characters in the *Recherche*. Swann has green eyes, red hair cut short. Odette is lovely, but her beauty is not to his taste—her profile is too marked, her skin too delicate, her cheekbones too prominent, her features too tightly drawn. Her eyes were lovely, but so large that they seemed to be bending under their own weight and straining the rest of her face. She has a superb figure, although it will later lose some of its slenderness, as her face will lose the expressive, sorrowful charm, the wide-eyed dreamy gaze she once had. Albertine has bright blue eyes, plump colorless cheeks, and a mass of black hair; in the beginning she is not the member of the band of girls who attracts him most, since she is brunette and his childhood encounter with Gilberte had left him with a taste for little girls with reddish hair and golden skin. Unlike Odette, Albertine, when she does come to attract him, does so because of her possession of remarkable reserves of vitality. She allows the protagonist a detailed knowledge of her body: "I opened her chemise. Her two little upstanding breasts were so round that they seemed not so much to be an integral part of her body as to have ripened there like fruit; and her belly . . . was closed, at the junction of her thighs, by two valves of a curve as hushed, as reposeful, as cloistral as that of the horizon after the sun has set."[6] He describes at length her beautiful legs, her full, strong neck. Like Odette, she loses her slender figure, and she is last seen as a very stout, mannish girl.

The body and its spatial location makes possible the further alienation constituted by the illusion of possession: "The possession of what one loves is an even greater joy than love itself."[7] But the narrator realizes, with regard to Albertine, that if her body was in the power of his, her thoughts escaped the grasp of his. He remarks that his joy at having possessed a little of her intelligence and her heart came not from their intrinsic value but from the belief that this possession was a further step in the total possession of her, which had been his goal and his chimera since the first day he had set eyes on her. But this sight of a physical body is elsewhere affirmed to be less then determining: "Generally speaking, love has not as its object a human body, except when an emotion, the fear of losing it, the uncertainty of finding it again have been infused into it."[8]

II *The Other as Mirror*

Various episodes reveal the importance, to the self, of the image it finds reflected in the eyes of the other. In order to ensure that this image is favorable, the self must often conform to a norm of conduct and evaluations which it must first strive to discern and grasp—so that it is forced ardently to seek its own alienation from spontaneous experience.

This is well illustrated by the young protagonist's conversion to admiration for the famous actress Berma, a conversion wrought not

by her performance, which on the contrary disappointed him, but
by the opinion of M. de Norpois and a newspaper critic. In reflecting upon the problem of insincerity which this situation raises,
the narrator concludes that all our ideas derive from each other, in
the course of their communal life in our mind, the strength they
need. Swann's relationship with Odette is characterized by the
functioning of a sort of "screen" of this type: jealousy interposed
between him and her a mass of suspicions developed in the past,
either in relation with Odette or with another, so that he could not
see her except through this veil. In a similar manner, it is the
reputation of the church of Balbec that helps the protagonist to appreciate it. Something similar again is true of his reaction at seeing
the Duchesse de Guermantes for the first time—but we shall return
to this example later; suffice it to say here that this deformation of
the self's reaction to others finds systematic expression in one of the
chief themes of the whole work, namely, that of snobbery. This
theme, brilliantly evoked in the early portrait of Legrandin, is
further developed in the description of the provincials at the Hôtel
de Balbec, and provides a great source of humor.

While we may well be struck by the quality of observation in the
narrative being developed, we must keep in mind that the narrator
prizes observation less than he does creation: "In the state of mind
in which we 'observe,' we are a long way below the level to which
we rise when we create."[9] Both this preference for creation and the
bracketing of the term "observe" warn us not to take too hastily the
view that all the narrator relates is observed rather than imagined.

Our dependence on that alienated form of knowledge of each
other which is constituted by visual observation is emphasized by
the continual reference to sight and gaze. "What a deceptive sense
sight is!" he declares, and often a character can only speculate on
the passionate thoughts hidden behind another's eyes, while at
other times a revealing gaze is turned away to hide its message.
Their eyes betray his mother's love, Françoise's cruelty, the hidden
intentions of an overanxious conspirator. An amusing passage is
devoted to the gaze which is framed by a monocle. The narrator
remarks of Albertine's eyes, which he calls "my regular infor-
mants": "Her blue, almond-shaped eyes, grown longer, had not
kept their form; they were indeed of the same colour, but seemed to
have passed into a liquid state. So much so that, when she shut
them it was as though a pair of curtains had been drawn to shut out
a view of the sea."[10] The protagonist's passion finds outlet in his

gaze, and he believes he can read a negative message in the pupils
of Albertine's eyes. A dominant category is that of the look in the
eyes of the homosexual—pederast, lesbian—looking for prey. The
special character of lesbian relations arouses both the fear and the
curiosity of the protagonist. At one point they are indicated by a
gaze reflected in a mirror, which provides an excellent symbol of
lesbianism, since homosexual relations are distinguished by their
mirror-image character: the other is stripped of otherness, and
becomes a mirror for the self.

The narrator tells us that at a certain point the girl he loved
among the members of the band at Balbec was Andrée. As we know
that Andrée is the main female alter ego of the protagonist, this is
actually an example of love of self.

The Other is a mirror for the Self partly because it remains impenetrable to the gaze, to the intelligence of the self, as is Odette to
Swann, Rachel to Saint-Loup, Albertine to the protagonist. The
narrator develops, in fact, a whole theory of relationships with the
other, others, and reality more generally, in which intuition is
declared to be superior to mere rational intelligence.[11] Intuitive understanding is represented by Françoise, of whom he declares that
she neither thought nor knew anything, and he remarks elsewhere:
"By dint of living with me and my parents her fears, her prudence,
her alertness, her cunning had ended by giving her that instinctive
and almost prophetic knowledge of us all that the mariner has of the
sea, the quarry of the hunter, and, of the malady, if not the physi-
cian, often at any rate the patient."[12] He has some doubts, however,
as to the exact nature of Françoise's penetration: he originally had
the impression that it was supernatural, so remarkable was it, but in
the end accepts the possibility that it was a matter of special means
of information.

In any case, he himself has a great respect and quite a taste for
nonrational understanding: he declares to Saint-Loup that he could
get quite enthusiastic about the art of warfare on the condition that
it resembled the other arts in being something more than a mere
learning of rules. He is delighted to learn that great generals allow
themselves to be guided by something very slight, perhaps based on
their experience but reinterpreted, and that Napoleon at times rejected all the rules to follow some obscure divination. The poetic
treasures conferred on things (and names) by the imagination are
quickly destroyed by the more "accurate," or at least realistic, information provided by the reductive and universalizing light of reason:

the charm of many place-names rapidly evaporates when Brichot explains their philological derivation.

The narrator has his revenge in the case of the interpretation of human behavior, where, he is convinced, rational analysis remains superficial and misleading. In art, likewise, the creative genius only reaches its greatest heights when it escapes from the method of elaboration developed by the rational intelligence, with its analytical orientation and ultimate superficiality. The narrator draws very broad and basic principles from these convictions: for him, the function of reasoning, as we learn from experience, is not to teach us those things which mean the most to us, for these come from other sources, but to collaborate with and serve these other sources.

III   *The Social Persona*

The distinction between the Other's social persona and more private personality clearly fascinates the narrator. He speculates on the transparency of this mask for Saint-Loup, "who, by an act of memory, beneath the indifference, transparent to him, of the motionless features which affected not to know him, or beneath the dull formality of the greeting that might equally well have been addressed to anyone else, could recall, could see, through dishevelled locks, a swooning mouth, a pair of half-closed eyes. . . ."[13] This voyeurism is a central characteristic of our narrator. A further veiling of reality is caused by the affected language of certain characters, such as Bloch or Legrandin, and the snobbery of others. The truth may be hidden from our eyes by intellectual dishonesty or hidden motives, which involve not merely the falsity of affectation but also deliberate concealment.

The narrator claims to have enjoyed extraordinary social success because of his intellectual and conversational brilliance, as in the scenes with the friends of Saint-Loup at Doncières, with Mme. Verdurin, with Albertine and her girl friends, with sundry aristocrats, or with the prettiest and most high-born debutante in Paris. He boasts of his younger self's numerous conquests, claiming fourteen in one season, reflects smugly on his superior social position, and evokes his tolerance, sweetness, disinterestedness, indulgence, and kindness toward Morel. The Duchesse de Guermantes pays him the compliment of appropriating his ideas and even his very words, and Saint-Loup, who considers himself vastly inferior to the protagonist, does the same. Andrée, who tells Elstir of her great liking for the protagonist, imitates his manner of speaking. He is proud of his influence on the intellectual development of Albertine, saying: "She is my work."[14]

He also quotes compliments paid to him by various characters. Saint-Loup refers to his sensitive nature and his hypersensitivity to sound, and says of his friends: "I have told them you are sublime"; he speaks of his "immense admiration" and declares: "You are the most intelligent man I know. . . . You are extraordinary."[15] Albertine exclaims: "Anybody would be delighted to live with you, just look how people run after you. They're always talking about you at Mme Verdurin's, and in high society too, I'm told."[16] He speaks of Albertine's prospects with him as representing for her "a brilliant marriage."

What distinguishes him particularly, besides his brilliance and sensitivity, is the fact that he belongs to what he calls "the Combray race, from which sprang absolutely unspoiled creatures like my grandmother and my mother."[17] This association of a character's social persona with a place or a domain is constant throughout the *Recherche*. It even occurs in connection with a character like Albertine, whom the protagonist associates with Balbec solely because he met her there. Marie Gineste and Céleste Albaret are seen as actual incarnations of the spirit of the mountain regions in which they were born and grew up. When surroundings are also possessions, the relationship is even more intimate. However, the most extreme tendency of the narrator in this direction manifests itself in relation to the aristocracy, with its geographically localized system of names. The narrator centers this first on the Duc and Duchesse de Guermantes: "This ducal personality was in its turn enormously distended, immaterialized, so as to encircle and contain that Guermantes of which they were duke and duchess, all that sunlit 'Guermantes way' of our walks, the course of the Vivonne, its water-lilies and its overshadowing trees, and an endless series of hot summer afternoons."[18] Other members of the aristocracy are also seen in this manner: the Prince of Faffenheim-Munsterburg-Weinigen is associated, through his name, with a little German watering place peopled with gnomes and undines and an enchanted mountain honored by the feet of Goethe upon which rose the ancient Burg that cherished memories of Luther and Lewis the Germanic; the name of the Princess of Parma contained the fragrance of thousands of violets and an atmosphere as stifling as a breathless summer

evening on the Piazza of a small town in Italy; the Duc
d'Agrigente's name appeared to the protagonist like a transparent
sheet of colored glass through which he beheld, struck, on the shore
of the violet sea, by the slanting rays of a golden sun, the rosy marble cubes of an ancient city; the Cambremer family members
appear garbed in the roof tiles of their castle or in the roughcast of
their parish church, their nodding heads barely reaching above the
vault of the nave or banqueting hall, and then only to cap
themselves with the Norman lantern or the dovecote of the pepper-
pot turret. Ultimately, disappointment comes, when the name is
replaced by the real person; but this movement from the ideal to
the real, from the sacred to the profane, is far from being the
"message" aimed at, the conclusion drawn.

IV   *People as Things*

The Sartrean view of the reduction of people to things by the
gaze of the other is primarily negative—a source of nausea. There
is, however, a positive side of such "reduction," and this is what the
Proustian narrator stresses most: the sense of sight, delegated by the
other senses, is directed at girls and gives them the same consistency
as when they plunder a rose garden or a vineyard whose clusters of
grapes they devour with their eyes. It is true that even in the
Recherche comparisons with plant life are not always flattering; but
they are nearly always so.

Comparisons of the whole of humanity to flowers are rare,
although we do find the occasional example. Almost invariably
floral comparisons are used for girls and women, and this in various
ways. They are used to illustrate the theme of reification, of woman
as inanimate: a midinette may have a nose whose quivering is as
devoid of meaning as that of a flower, and Albertine reminds him of
a long blossoming stem—as though by falling asleep she had
become a plant. The comparison may suggest mystery, as when Andrée is described as resembling a strange, dark flower that was
brought to him from beyond the grave. Mostly, however, flowers
suggest beauty: he finds flower maidens and flower ladies not only
at Balbec but also in the streets of Paris and in the salon of the
Guermantes. Albertine is a seaside rose whose cheeks have
flowerlike flesh-tints, replacing in his life the admiration for Odette,
"the most beautiful flower," and Oriane, "the most curious flower
of the season." Swann hovers over the magnificent bosom of Mme.

de Surgis like a butterfly over a flower, and the sexualization of the flower symbol (and of the assimilation of flower and woman) through the traditional notion of defloration finds expression in the phrase spoken by Swann to Odette: "do a cattleya." Letters received from women are described as "lovely flowers," while spoken language *(parole)* is distinguished from written *(écriture)* by its being enhanced by diffusion over "the expanded water-lily of the face." The flavor of the narrator's floral imagery is perhaps best suggested by the following succulent passage: "Suddenly, on the gravelled path, unhurrying, cool, luxuriant, Mme Swann appeared, displaying around her a toilet which was never twice the same, but which I remember as being typically mauve; then she hoisted and unfurled at the end of its long stalk, just at the moment when her radiance was most complete, the silken banner of a wide parasol of a shade that matched the showering petals of her gown."[19]

Women are sometimes equated not with flowers but with landscapes. This may at times be little more than a mere matter of imagery, as in the description of a change in Odette's facial expression, which he compares to a grey countryside, covered with clouds which suddenly disperse, to permit its transfiguration, at the moment the sun sets. Even this has perhaps more than a merely decorative function; the relating of woman to landscape usually goes far deeper, reflecting a basic fact of the narrator's view of reality. An intimate relationship, almost a mode of symbiosis, is postulated between a woman and the landscape to which she belongs. Perhaps the most remarkable passage of this type is the following, which occurs early in the work: "But to wander thus among the woods of Roussainville without a peasant-woman to embrace was to see those woods and yet know nothing of their secret treasure, their deep-hidden beauty. That girl whom I never saw save dappled with the shadows of their leaves, was to me herself a plant of local growth, only taller than the rest, and one whose structure would enable me to approach more closely than in them to the intimate savour of the land from which she had sprung."[20]

Several variations are possible. Whereas here the landscape is real, the woman fictitious, a real landscape may be accompanied by a real (if still unknown and unnamed) woman, as in the case of the peasant milkmaid encountered in the course of a train journey. In other cases, both woman and landscape are real and familiar; thus he says of Albertine: "I felt that it was possible for me, on the girl's two cheeks, to kiss the whole of the beach at Balbec"; and of

Gilberte and Oriane: "The shadow of Gilberte lay, not only before a church in the Ile-de-France where I had pictured her to myself, but also on the path of a park along the Méséglise way, and the shadow of Mme de Guermantes in a moist roadway where red and violet clusters rose in spikes, or else over the golden morning brightness of a Parisian sidewalk."[21] Finally, this theme is developed in connection with a woman who is known and a landscape which is imagined: Andrée has facial features from the Midi, vocal tones from Périgord; Rosemonde has the appearance and prankish temperament of the Northern provinces. The most striking example of the last case is provided by the narrator's view of Mlle de Stermaria: "In her romantic Breton castle, we should perhaps have been able to wander by ourselves at evening, she and I together in the dusk which would shew in a softer light above the darkening water pink briar roses, beneath oak trees beaten and stunted by the hammering of the waves. . . . For it seemed to me that I should not really have possessed her save there, when I should have traversed those regions which enveloped her in so many memories."[22]

The comparison of girls to flowers has an old-world flavor about it—its charm does not come from any imaginative achievement of originality, but rather from its exquisite elaboration. Comparisons with localities are already more striking (although even these are not unique to Proust; one thinks of Verlaine's well-known verse: "Votre âme est un paysage choisi"). Other comparisons made by the Proustian narrator are, however, effectively unexpected. Parts (the *stamina*) of certain plants look like insects transformed into flowers. The image of a moth or butterfly is used to describe a ray of sunshine, a ship, the nostrils of Robert and of Swann. The narrator compares himself to a bee, and the Prince d'Agrigente and above all M. d'Argencourt in old age are compared to insects. Several characters are compared to birds, including the protagonist, a waiter, a young milkmaid, Mme Verdurin, more frequently Albertine, and above all Oriane.

At a further stage of metamorphosis, in which the change in appearance is replaced by a change from life to lifelessness, people are seen not as living animals, which at least are still "natural," but as artificial constructs, works of art. Just as memory will reduce the real Combray and make its streets appear even more unreal than the projections of the magic lantern, so history can reduce real people like the Duke and Duchess of Guermantes to the status of fictions: "Whenever I thought about them I pictured them to myself either in tapestry, as was the 'Coronation of Esther' which hung in our church, or else in changing, rainbow colours, as was Gilbert the Bad in his window, where he passed from cabbage green, when I was dipping my fingers in the holy water stoup, to plum blue when I had reached our row of chairs, or again altogether impalpable, like the image of Geneviève de Brabant, ancestress of the Guermantes family, which the magic lantern sent wandering over the curtains of my room or flung aloft upon the ceiling."[23] Sculpture is used to evoke the faces of the aging Alix and of the protagonist's dead or dying grandmother. Both Robert and Oriane are compared to statues, as are Morel and above all Albertine, whose peasant charm is reflected in the statues of old country churches. The narrator writes of Theodore that when he raised Aunt Léonie's head on the pillow he had the naïve and zealous look of the little angels in low reliefs, thronging, taper in hand, about the deathbed of Our Lady; and a peasant girl encountered in the church porch is a replica of the statue of a saint which had "the full cheeks, the firm breasts which swelled inside her draperies like a cluster of ripe grapes inside a bag, the narrow forehead, short and stubborn nose, deep-set eyes, and strong, thick-skinned, courageous expression of the country-women of those parts."[24]

Famous artists are sometimes used to provide visual indications. Thus an aging beauty had the figure of a goddess by Coysevox, a young salesgirl is a Titian. Albertine strikes the protagonist as less beautiful than female figures by Veronese, and appears as unreal as figures by Benozzo Gozzoli; at one point she reminds him of a figure by Giotto—or she pretends to be as deaf as a portrait by La Tour. Swann sees in various servants diverse figures from works by Mantegna, Goya, or Cellini; he compares a woman with a portrait by Luini or her costume to a painting by Giorgione; he sees in the scullery maid Giotto's *Charity* and in M. de Palancy Giotto's *Un-just*, and Odette reminds him of a Botticelli.

Finally, people may become fictions partly through the costumes they wear. Albertine is particularly interested in this mute language of dresses, but the narrator sees this interest as quite general, and remarks at one point that in the lives of most women everything, even the greatest sorrow, resolves itself into a question of trying on new clothes. The first important character from this point of view is Odette, who creates a veritable myth around her by her choice of clothes, and indeed it is doubtful whether her portrait is ever surpassed later. At first, we are told that the fashion of the moment made women look as if they were made up of different pieces badly fitted together, but later that "Odette seemed now to be cut out in a single figure, wholly confined within a line which, following the contours of the woman, had abandoned the winding paths, the capricious re-entrants and salients, the radial points, the elaborate dispersions of the fashions of former days.''[25] There follow sumptuous evocations of her clothes, whether worn at home or for strolling in public places. The narrator remarks that she seemed to dress not merely for the convenience or adornment of her body but to surround herself with the most delicate manifestation of a civilization. Later it will be Oriane who represents the lady of fashion, and her influence upon the taste of the protagonist is reflected in the wardrobe of Albertine, Oriane's love for the creations of Fortuny being shared by both Albertine and the protagonist.

When the outward-bound self at last reaches the realm of social intercourse, it may be thought that experience of real others would at last be achieved; this, however, is an illusion. The first impact of society is the imposition of interlocking codes of conduct which dictate artificial modes of being that alienate the self from authentic, immediate experience of reality. Interpersonal relationships are found to be dependent on social and financial status or purely external, physical beauty, thus corrupting both others and self. Gradually the self learns to see all reality—an actress, a mistress, a church—through a screen of criteria provided by society. (The only way to counter this alienating influence is to reject rational intelligence in favor of intuition—which the narrator does, at least on the theoretical level.)

The social persona, which is reflected in such elements as choice of language, is adopted as a means of concealing one's more private personality (which might be less socially acceptable). The protagonist's persona is represented as much sought after: he combines intellectual brilliance with the sensitivity and purity typical of Combray. This association of social persona with geographical locality is applied constantly to other characters also. Furthermore, individuals are seen not only as emanations of places and domains but also as plants, flowers, insects, fish, and birds, or as works of sculpture or painting. Metamorphosis may even be deliberately sought after, as in the passion for gorgeous clothes shown by Odette, Oriane, and Albertine. All of these disguises and associations are manifestations of the artificiality of the social persona, and of the alienated character inherent in social discourse.

CHAPTER 5

Things

I *Things and Sensations: Their Subjective Character*

WHEN we read the *Recherche*, one of the first aspects that strike us is the role of a number of concrete objects: a cake, a paving-stone, some church steeples, a clump of trees, a musical phrase, even a chamber pot. There are several reasons for our being attracted by these objects. One is the remarkable texture which they possess or which is given to them by their manner of representation. Another is the rich store of associations they involve, imply, and at times release, determining the role they play or are made to play in their particular context.

Constantly, throughout the *Recherche*, relationships are constructed in which greater levels, dimensions, or forms of life are implied by smaller. Odette's parasol will be seen as "open and outstretched like another, a nearer sky, round, clement, mobile, blue."[1] And vice versa: the sky looks like a swimming pool filled with blue water. The bedroom of the beginning, with its Chinese lantern shadows and its relationship with the mother, is a microcosm for the larger episode of *Swann's Way*, which similarly involves an obsessive relationship with a woman against a background series of portraits, beyond which there is the relative macrocosm of the whole work, with its many characters and the relationship with Albertine, while the ultimate macrocosm is the life of Man and his relationship with Woman and a multitude of Others.

Attention is drawn to this microcosmic-macrocosmic significance by means of a number of structural elements. The following passage develops this point: "It is true that my quarrels with Françoise and Albertine, had been merely private quarrels, which involved only the life of one little spiritual cell, namely, a human being. But, just as there are animal bodies and human bodies, that is to say, combinations of cells each of which, as compared with a single cell, is as big as a mountain, in the same way there are huge organized agglomerations of individuals, which are called 'nations'; their existence simply repeats on an amplified scale the existence of the component cells, and whoever is unable to comprehend the mystery, the reactions and the laws of the latter, will utter only empty words when he comes to speak of struggles between nations."[2] Among the most striking are the instances where such small and insignificant objects as a cake or a chamber pot are made to release—shown to contain, or at least to refer to, to imply—a whole world because of certain relationships stored in the narrator's memory and imagination.

Our tendency to construct the world around us is evoked a number of times. We attribute souls to things we see. In connection with illusions concerning people, for example, the narrator remarks: "We are all of us obliged, if we are to make reality endurable, to nurse a few little follies in ourselves."[3] A particularly striking illusion is that of stability: "On each occasion a girl so little resembles what she was the time before . . . that the stability of nature which we ascribe to her is purely fictitious and a convenience of speech."[4] This illusion of motionlessness is also evoked in connection with the observation of natural but nonpersonal objects, such as clouds. Such constant flux is as threatening to us as forgetfulness. The effort not to forget people and things is "a secret, partial, tangible and true aspect of our resistance to death."[5] These illusions are the product of an ineradicable subjectivity: "Only superficial and defective observation attaches all importance to the object, when the mind is everything,"[6] and "the universe is true for all of us and dissimilar to each of us."[7] As the narrator remarks, it is not only the physical world which differs from the way we see it: all reality may well be just as different from its appearance, which we ourselves elaborate by means of unconsciously held ideas. One aspect of our misconstruction of the universe is represented by the illusions entertained in us by people's lies.

The subjective character of the protagonist's relationship with things is reflected in an extremely anthropomorphic view of them. He speaks of "my neighbour, the countryside" in "her sweet morning robe of fog" which she soon takes off, and observes "a meager hill," saying: "I could not take my eyes from this stranger who, too, was looking at me for the first time."[8] Even odors are treated as quasi-human creatures: he speaks of "smells natural enough indeed, and coloured by circumstances as are those of the neighbouring countryside, but already humanized, domesticated, confined, an exquisite, skillful, limpid jelly, blending all the fruits of the season which have left the orchard for the store-room, smells changing with the year, but plenishing, domestic smells, which compensate for the sharpness of hoar frost with the sweet savour of warm bread, smells lazy and punctual as a village clock, roving smells, pious smells: rejoicing in a peace which serves as a deep source of poetry to the stranger who passes through those rooms without having lived amongst them."[9]

The elements are treated in a similar fashion: he speaks of "the waves that threw themselves forward like divers on a springboard," and of the sea's waves of emerald stone polished and translucid here and there, to which he attributes a placid violence, a leonine frown, and a faceless smile bestowed by the sun. He evokes the wind as the very spirit of Combray, and sees it come to lie at his feet, warm and murmuring. Of the fire in Saint-Loup's room, he remarks: "I felt that the room was not empty, that there must be somebody there. But it was only the freshly lighted fire beginning to burn. It could not keep quiet, it kept shifting its faggots about, and very clumsily. I entered the room; it let one roll into the fender and set another smoking. And even when it was not moving, like an ill-bred person it made noises all the time, . . . although if I had been on the other side of a wall I should have thought that they came from some one who was blowing his nose and walking about."[10] These sounds eventually die down: "The fire . . . had at length grown accustomed to the grate, and, like an animal crouching in an ardent, noiseless, faithful watchfulness, let fall only now and then a smouldering log which crumbled into sparks, or licked with a tongue of flame the sides of the chimney."[11] The element which undergoes the most frequent and significant anthropomorphosis is the sun, but its evocation is part of a broader movement which it is important to observe. Whereas such references to the sun abound in the first volumes (*Swann's Way*, *Within a Budding Grove*), they tend to be replaced thereafter by reference to the golden syllables of the Guermantes name (especially in *The Guermantes Way*) and the evocation of the sunlike golden hair of the Guermantes family.

At Combray, the narrator remarks that in the morning the winter sun had come to warm itself in front of the fire, while in the afternoon "a reflection of the sunlight had contrived to slip in on its golden wings, remaining motionless, between glass and woodwork, in a corner, like a butterfly poised upon a flower."[12] At Balbec he

says of the sea that "the sun spread itself here and there like a lazy
giant who might at any moment come leaping down their craggy
sides . . . until, dizzy with its sublime excursion over the thunder-
ing and chaotic surface of their crests and avalances, it came back to
take shelter from the wind in my bedroom, swaggering across the
unmade bed and scattering its riches over the splashed surface of
the basin-stand, and into my open trunk, where by its very splen-
dour and ill-matched luxury, it added still further to the general
effect of disorder."[13]

From *The Guermantes Way* onward, this particularly striking
type of evocation of the sun tends to disappear, but we find a new
stress on the Guermantes, who are surrogates of the sun. The
emphasis is first placed on the Guermantes name, "the legendary,
amaranthine name," and on what its brilliant orange envelope contains; he stresses "this amaranthine colour of the last syllable of her
name [containing] aspects of yellowing woods and a whole
mysterious little country region," and refers again later to "the
golden-syllabled name." There is increasing reference to the
blondness of the Guermantes, such as the young Marquis de
Beausergent but more especially Oriane and Robert. The latter's
blondness is explicitly identified as solar in character: we are told
that his skin was as blond and his hair as golden as if they had absorbed all the rays of the sun, and the narrator refers to "the colour
which was his more than all the other Guermantes', to be simply the
sunshine of a golden day solidified."[14] This quality is, however,
shared with the whole of the Guermantes family, as we see from the
description of the Baron de Guermantes and the Duc de
Chatellerault: "Tall, slender, with golden hair and sunny complex-
ions, thoroughly of the Guermantes type, these two young men
looked like a condensation of the light of the spring evening which
was flooding the spacious room."[15]

II *Interpenetration with Reality*

The narrator complains of the impossibility of escaping from his
own Self and of making meaningful contact with external reality,
but such contact is clearly more possible for such a consciousness
than for almost any other: what work of literature ever gave a more
striking impression of the mutual permeability of subject and object, narrator and world?

As the narrating consciousness moves out from itself toward the

world of phenomena, it identifies with the latter: "I had been thinking all the time, while I was asleep, of what I had just been reading,
but my thoughts had run into a channel of their own, until I myself
seemed actually to have become the subject of my book: a church, a
quartet, the rivalry between François I and Charles V."[16] To a lesser
but still vitally significant degree, this identification with objects
lasts throughout the work—or rather, it takes the form of a
relationship, whether of sympathy or of hostility, so intense that it
creates a permeating atmosphere of easy empathy and rich comparison, almost of transmigration (of the narrator's consciousness
into its material environment) such that all reality is woven into one
glistening web in whose center the magic spinner takes its place at
the last, part and parcel, source and cause, explanation and key to
the wondrous verbal artifact spread out in shifting lights and shades
to catch our dazzled minds.

Some objects, of course, are themselves of such a nature as to
lend themselves to imaginative enlivenment, especially when the
observer's emotional circumstances are propitious. Hence it is that
the narrator writes of the rings Albertine has accepted from an unknown admirer (and therefore a rival to the protagonist):
"Thunderstruck, holding the two rings in my hand, I stared at that
pitiless eagle whose beak was rending my heart, whose wings,
chiselled in high relief, had borne away the confidence that I re-
tained in my mistress, in whose claws my tortured mind was unable
to escape for an instant from the incessantly recurring questions."[17]

More often, however, the objects with which this type of imaginative link is established are in themselves not thus symbolic but
relatively neutral, and the narrator is aware of this: we alone can, by
our belief that they have an independent existence, give certain
things we see a soul which they keep thenceforth and develop in us.
Nevertheless, this awareness is far from exorcising the spirit or consciousness attributed to his material surroundings:

It is our noticing them that puts things in a room, our growing used to
them that takes them away again and clears a space for us. Space there was
none for me in my bedroom (mine in name only) at Balbec; it was full of
things which did not know me, which flung back at me the distrustful look
that I had cast at them, and, without taking any heed of my existence,
shewed that I was interrupting the course of theirs. The clock—whereas at
home I heard my clock tick only a few seconds in a week, when I was coming out of some profound meditation—continued without a moment's in-

terruption to utter, in an unknown tongue, a series of observations which must have been most uncomplimentary to myself, for the violet curtains listened to them without replying but in an attitude such as people adopt who shrug their shoulders to indicate that the sight of a third person irritates them.[18]

This impression of hostility gradually disappears, and he feels comfort in the presence which at first seemed so hostile. Others besides the protagonist see old friends ("a thing . . . is almost a person") in places, furniture, even antique cutlery: Françoise, Oriane, the Verdurins; but this syndrome is at its strongest in the protagonist himself. When his family moves to an apartment which is attached to the Hôtel de Guermantes, he remarks: "Like a boa constrictor that has just swallowed an ox, I felt myself painfully distended by the sight of a long trunk which my eyes had still to digest."[19] When he goes to visit Saint-Loup and thinks he will have to stay at a local hotel, he reflects that, no matter how pretty a place was, if it was new to him it caused him an anguish as painful as that experienced years ago at Combray when his mother did not come to kiss him good-night or that which he had felt the first day of his arrival at Balbec in the high-ceilinged room which smelled of flowering grasses.

He is mistaken, however: what he finds in this hotel is "lobbies as long as corridors and as ornate as drawing-rooms, which had the air rather of being dwellers there themselves than of forming part of a dwelling, which could not be induced to enter and settle down in any of the rooms but wandered about outside mine and came up at once to offer me their company—neighbours of a sort, idle but never noisy, menial ghosts of the past who had been granted the privilege of staying, provided they kept quiet, by the doors of the rooms which were let to visitors, and who, every time that I came across them, greeted me with a silent deference."[20] His reaction to this (imaginary) friendliness of a place is as lively as it is to its imaginary hostility: "When I came to the end, the bare wall in which no door opened said to me simply: 'Now you must turn and go back, but you see, you are at home here, the house is yours,' while the soft carpet, not to be left out, added that if I did not sleep that night I could easily come in barefoot, and the unshuttered windows, looking out over the open country, assured me that they would hold a sleepless vigil and that, at whatever hour I chose to come in, I need not be afraid of disturbing anyone. And behind a hanging curtain I surprised only a little closet which, stopped by the wall and unable to escape any farther, had hidden itself there with a guilty conscience and gave me a frightened stare from its little round window, glowing blue in the moonlight.''[21]

The protagonist's imagination animates not only objects and places but even time: he describes the grey day as tired and resigned, stitching its shimmering needlework and as inattentive to him as a preoccupied seamstress.

All of these examples of the tendency to inject "spirit" into the inanimate seem to reflect a conviction of the universal oneness of all things—a conviction which manifests itself, for instance, in his reflections on his unrequited love for the Duchesse de Guermantes: he consoles himself with the thought that it is a tiny fragment of universal love. Mutual permeability is essential to human relations, as we see from how little a person is when he or she is no longer, or not yet, permeable to our emotions. Because of this mutual permeability of impressions, the memory of Albertine brings with it many others: "From the sound of the rain I recaptured the scent of the lilacs at Combray, from the shifting of the sun's rays on the balcony the pigeons in the Champs-Elysées, from the muffling of all noise in the heat of the morning hours, the cool taste of cherries, the longing for Brittany or Venice from the sound of the wind and the return of Easter.''[22] This permeability seems, in fact, to the narrator, inevitable—after having seemed impossible: the monologue of the soul which believes it is imprisoned in itself is not really a monologue at all, for it is modified by external reality.

One of the most striking images of the manner in which the narrating consciousness espouses objects and molds itself to phenomena is provided by Golo, the magic-lantern hero, who will turn out to be a surrogate for the narrator: "If the lantern were moved I could still distinguish Golo's horse advancing across the window-curtains, swelling out with their curves and diving into their folds. The body of Golo himself, being of the same supernatural substance as his steed's, overcame all material obstacles—everything that seemed to bar his way—by taking each as it might be a skeleton and embodying it in himself: the door-handle, for instance, over which, adapting itself at once, would float invincibly his red cloak or his pale face, never losing its nobility or its melancholy, never showing any sign of trouble at such a transubstantiation.''[23] This idea is repeated later in connection with the glassed bookshelves which reflected the sea in the hotel room at

Balbec: "The round red sun had already sunk halfway down the slanting sheet of glass, which formerly I had detested, and, like a Greek fire, was inflaming the sea in the glass fronts of all my book-cases."[24]

III   *Transformation and Transcendence*

The encounter with overtly insignificant objects and events is sufficient to provoke in our protagonist all kinds of visions, memories, comparisons, reflections, generalizations. The most striking of such experiences are presented as very special, and as belonging to the nonrational, nonintellectual domain of involuntary memory: such an event, with its sense of wonder and delight and its myriad, almost magical ramifications, is described at the end of the first section of the first book, and the phenomenon involved deserves close attention. But this phenomenon is by no means isolated. It is related to many other experiences; and the nature of this relationship is indicated by the structure of this first section, which the episode of the little cake serves to close. The transfiguration of the real, the simple, the banal, by involuntary memory constitutes the final, highest level of such transformation, a kind of climax, which must be understood in terms of its relationship to other levels of the same effect.

The best proof of this lies in the fact that if the taste of the cake evokes Combray, it is not the first experience to do so: Combray is recalled and evoked much earlier, if less vividly, by a position adopted when lying in bed. This experience provokes the following thirty-five pages devoted to the narrator's life at Combray. The episode of the madeleine constitutes a recapitulation, on a higher level of intensity, of the first six pages of the work, and initiates a movement of transcendence which culminates in the evocation of the church of Saint-Hilaire, its bell-tower and its steeple, elements of verticality which are prolonged by the flights of birds which rise even higher into the air and finally by the transfiguration of the whole heaven-bent structure in the enveloping rays of the setting sun: "And when she gazed on it, when her eyes followed the gentle tension, the fervent inclination of its stony slopes, which drew together as they rose, like hands joined in prayer, she would absorb herself so utterly in the outpouring of the spire that her gaze seemed to leap upwards with it; her lips at the same time curving in a friendly smile for the worn old stones of which the setting sun now illumined no more than the topmost pinnacles, which, at the point where they entered that zone of sunlight and were softened and sweetened by it, seemed to have mounted suddenly far higher, to have become truly remote, like a song whose singer breaks into falsetto, an octave above the accompanying air."[25]

The church is made to suggest transcendence in several other ways also. For instance, it is associated with winged creatures—the "huge stone bat" of the crypt, the multitude of crows inhabiting the steeple—which traditionally symbolize the abandonment of earthly things, the ability to rise above them. The bell-towers suggest transcendence not only through their verticality but also through the symbolism of the bell, suspended above the earth.

Furthermore, the sun, when associated with the church, sometimes appears to have a mysterious, even mystical quality, being described as "invisible" when it illuminates the tapestries and paradoxically "black" when it strikes the slate roof at the base of the steeple.

The notion of transformation, introduced from the very first pages of the work through the child's magic lantern, is repeated again several times. Reference is made to a large party with a Chinese lantern show given by the Princesse de Parme. The narrator records that when sleeping he visualized imaginary spectacles upon the screen of his sleep. Transformation is often a matter of lighting: "In a little curiosity shop a candle, burned almost to its socket, projecting its warm glow over an engraving reprinted it in sanguine, while, battling against the darkness, the light of the big lamp tanned a scrap of leather, inlaid a dagger with fiery spangles, on pictures which were only bad copies spread a priceless film of gold like the patina of time or the varnish used by a master, made in fact of the whole hovel, in which there was nothing but pinchbeck rubbish, a marvelous composition by Rembrandt."[26] The mind of the artist is like a magic lantern: "The parts of the wall that were covered by paintings from his brush, all homogeneous with one another, were like the luminous images of a magic lantern, which would have been in this instance the brain of the artist, and the strangeness of which one could never have suspected so long as one had known only the man, which was like seeing the iron lantern boxing its lamp before any coloured slide had been slid into its groove."[27] Reality is often less authentic in appearance than illusion: "A great designer will procure a far more sumptuous impression by focussing a ray of light on a doublet of coarse cloth studded

with lumps of glass and on a cloak of paper."[28] The narrator speaks
of the successive form of the hours when he had seen Albertine, a
form which remained that of his memory just as the curve of the
projections of his magic lantern resulted from the curve of the
colored pieces of glass. Dreams also, of course, are illusions.

Like Shakespeare, he stresses the fact that the world (for example,
of society) is merely a vaster theater, and Albertine strikes him as a
great actress of the sunstruck beach, exciting jealousies when she
appeared on this natural theater, speaking to no one, dominating
her friends.

The notion of transformation is further enriched by certain striking images used by the narrator: "The motionless wings of vessels,
smoky blue in the distance, looked like exotic and nocturnal moths
in a show-case"; "At once I saw her gelatinous features change.
Like a syrup that has turned, her face seemed permanently
clouded": "On certain fine days the weather was so cold, one was in
such full communication with the street that it seemed as though a
breach had been made in the outer walls of the house, and,
whenever a tramcar passed, the sound of its bell throbbed like that
of a silver knife striking a wall of glass. But it was most of all in
myself that I heard, with intoxication, a new sound rendered by the
hidden violin. Its strings are tightened or relaxed by mere changes
of temperature, of light, in the world outside."

Transformation by personification is not uncommon: he speaks of
the Vivonne murmuring like a person whispering, and describes as
follows the moon and a nearby star: "The moon was now in the sky
like a section of orange delicately peeled although slightly bruised.
But presently she was to be fashioned of the most enduring gold.
Sheltering alone behind her, a poor little star was to serve as sole
companion to the lonely moon, while she, keeping her friend
protected, but bolder and striding ahead, would brandish like an
irresistible weapon, like an Oriental symbol, her broad and
marvellous crescent of gold."[29] Paris is transformed into some exotic
foreign city such as Venice: "It is of its poorer quarters that certain
poor quarters of Paris make one think, in the morning, with their
tall, wide chimneys to which the sun imparts the most vivid pinks,
the brightest reds; it is a whole garden that flowers above the
houses, and flowers in such variety of tints that one would call it,
planted on top of the town, the garden of a tulip-fancier of Delft or
Haarlem."[30]

Aquatic images are used several times. Thus Swann says to

Odette: "You are a formless water that will trickle down any slope that it may come upon, a fish devoid of memory, incapable of thought, which all its life long in its aquarium will continue to dash itself, a hundred times a day, against a wall of glass, always mistaking it for water."[31] A character may suggest a fish: M. de Palancy and the Princesse de Luxembourg are both compared to carp, and we are told of the former that "the Marquis de Palancy, his face bent downwards at the end of his long neck, his round bulging eye glued to the glass of his monocle, was moving with a leisurely displacement through the transparent shade and appeared no more to see the public in the stalls than a fish that drifts past, unconscious of the press of curious gazers, behind the glass wall of an aquarium."[32] A similar image is suggested by the view from the street into lighted apartments "in which amphibious men and women floated slowly to and fro in the rich liquid that after nightfall rose incessantly from the wells of the lamps."[33] The narrator compares the invisible wall which separates the blind lover from public opinion concerning his beloved to a glass partition as impervious to such conversations as the walls of an aquarium to those of strollers who pass by. The denizens of earth and sea appear to be interchangeable: a huge marine monster will seem a multicolored cathedral of the sea, while two ancient bell-towers, covered in salmon-pink tiles, look like old fish swimming motionlessly in transparent blue water.

Two of the most richly developed transformations worked by the mind of the narrator are aquatic in character; they concern the dining room of the Grand Hôtel de Balbec and the *loge* of the Guermantes at the opera. The dining room, which seems now an immense aviary, now a system of planets and stars, mostly takes on the appearance of a huge aquarium: "an important social question, this: whether the wall of glass will always protect the wonderful creatures at their feasting, whether the obscure folk who watch them hungrily out of the night will not break in some day to gather them from their aquarium and devour them."[34] This image is extended to include the adjacent garden, which looks like "the vegetation of a pale and green aquarium of gigantic size seen by a supernatural light."[35] There is also a reminiscence much later, when he recalls "the dining-room at Balbec in the evening, with, on the other side of the windows, all that populace crowded together in the dusk, as before the luminous glass of an aquarium."[36]

If *Within a Budding Grove* is thus ornamented by the watery transformation of the dining room into an aquarium, the following

volume, *The Guermantes Way*, opens with a sumptuous transformation of the *baignoire* (opera-box) of the Guermantes into an un-
dersea grotto: "The passage to which he was directed after mentioning the word *baignoire*, and along which he now proceeded,
was moist and mildewed and seemed to lead to subaqueous grot-
toes, to the mythical kingdom of the water-nymphs."[37] The narrator
evokes the white goddesses who inhabited these shadowy abodes,
and the dark and transparent kingdom ringed by the limpid and
reflecting eyes of the water-spirits: "The radiant daughters of the
sea kept turning at every moment to smile up at the bearded tritons
who clung to the anfractuosities of the cliff, or towards some aquatic
demi-god, whose head was a polished stone to which the tides had
borne a smooth covering of sea-weed, and his gaze a disc of rock
crystal."[38] The queen of this underworld domain is Oriane de Guermantes, whose rank and affiliation are indicated by her costume of
seashells and pearls, and the members of the Jockey Club are sacred
sea monsters floating in the depths of the cave. As with the dining
room, there will be later reminiscences of this aquatic manifestation.

Whereas the transformation of the dining room into an aquarium
full of fish is a downward modification, that of the inhabitants of
the *loge* into gods and goddesses of the deep is clearly upward,
enhancing mere transformation by means of a clear suggestion of
transcendence of the earthly (let alone the animal) realm by the
supernatural in the form of the mythological.

IV   *The Magic of Metamorphosis*

Not only does the narrating consciousness permeate external
phenomena and vice versa, but its manner of perceiving such
phenomena is such that they are seen in a constant flux of
metamorphosis. Human qualities may be attributed to things,
plants, trees. Flowers may be compared with insects, asparagus with
a fairy; the sky is "as big as a wild animal," the sun is tamed into a
domestic pet, and the tranquil pond is described as "asleep."

The importance given throughout the work to relationship with
and alienation from Self and Other, persons and things gives a certain significance (through participation in this theme) to even so
relatively banal an element as the disorientation caused by the long
walks around Combray. This disorientation derives further interest
from its function of illustrating the central interpersonal triad

Father-Mother-Son: it is organized by the Father, who alone possesses the key to the labyrinth of paths traversed and who at the end triumphantly and ironically exploits it to reaffirm his superiority; it confirms the Mother in her admiration for the Father; and the young initiate gratefully welcomes the return to a more familiar reality as a comforting Return to the Womb: "Custom came to take me in her arms, carried me all the way up to my bed, and laid me down there like a little child."[39]

The phenomenal world is seen as ephemeral and unreal; surviving only in memory and originally invented by the observer's perceptions, belief in this world of appearances—a perfume of flowers along a hedge, the sound of a step on a gravel path, a bubble clinging to a plant in the stream—distinguishes the boy who wandered through the Combray countryside in an ecstasy of enthusiasm from the older narrator who has lost this gift of immediate sensibility: "It is because I used to believe in things, in people, when I was roaming among them, that the things, the people they taught me to know, and those alone, I still take seriously, still give me joy. Whether it be that the faith which creates has ceased to exist in me, or that reality will take shape in the memory alone, the flowers that people show me nowadays for the first time do not seem to me to be real flowers."[40]

Things are porous for such a mind: it steals into them, just as it allows them to permeate it through their colors, odors, and even attitudes. Things usually provide a treasured atmosphere of familiarity, but such is the narrator's exquisite sensitivity to their intimate and active role in his life that he may at times find them hostile and adopt an attitude of hatred for them. His mood so dominates his view of reality that the latter appears to conform to his state of mind. This dissolution of the barriers between the internal and external worlds, between the psychological and the material, is such that odors, for example, among the most elusive of sense-experiences, are hated or lovingly appreciated as participating in both the material and the moral spheres. Feelings and motives, as well as things, are likewise lovingly and humorously enumerated, like interesting stones of varied hue, shape, and texture that one allows to slip slowly through one's fingers.

Plants have a life of their own: he evokes the huge chrysanthemums Odette has in her living room at the beginning of the winter, which reproduce the hues of November sunsets in the remarkable beauty and variety of their coloring—they are "rose-pale like the Louis XV silk that covered her chairs, snow-white like her *crêpe-de-Chine* wrapper, or of a metallic red like her samovar."[41] The protagonist finds the hawthorns, his favorite flowers, more mysterious and more interesting than living people; he remarks of flowers that Elstir is painting that they are not of the sort he would rather see portrayed than people—hawthorns, cornflowers, apple-blossom.

What, then, are the flowers favored in the *Recherche?* Odette shows Swann an orchid with a particular esteem, as for an elegant sister provided for her by nature, more worthy of finding a place in her salon than many women. The protagonist's favorite flowers are the hawthorns and the flowering fruit trees—apple, cherry, pear. All are transformed into women and girls. Sometimes an even more dramatic transformation takes place: the Orient, which will later be evoked by the narrator to transform Venice and finally even Paris, is used by him to express the poesy of the buttercups, and the flowering fruit trees in all their splendor are likened to angels and strange gods.

As the narrator remarks, "our mind is the old Proteus".[42]

Material objects play a role in the *Recherche* that is both rich and strange. They are related to the vast universe as microcosm to macrocosm; they are transformed by imagination and anthropomorphosis, symbolized by the magic lantern. The elements are frequently viewed thus—fire, the sea, above all the sun. The narrator projects upon inanimate reality the symbiotic fusion he has with his mother: rooms and furniture are endowed with their own, highly individualized personalities, usually hostile until familiar. This transformation of banal, everyday reality is most dramatically effected by memory, especially certain cases of involuntary recall, and these are associated with symbols of transcendence—birds, church spires. A veritable apotheosis is suggested by the evocation of the Guermantes and their friends in the guise of aquatic deities. Plants, flowers, and flowering trees are likewise metamorphosed into familiar friends or supernatural beings. Thus the narrator's symbiotic fusion with all of reality leads to the dissolution of the conventional frontiers between the various levels of being, the human fusing with the subhuman and the superhuman in a vast and seamless unity.

CHAPTER 6

Symbols

I *Farms, Trees, and Bell-Towers*

WHILE many commentators have analyzed the role given to involuntary memory in the system developed by the Proustian narrator, and the relationship between such memory and art, there are other obscure impressions, as the narrator himself points out,[1] which attract his attention not because of past experiences they recall but because of future truths they seem to promise. The most striking of these impressions—those emanating from the three farms,[2] the three trees,[3] and above all the three bell towers[4]—have a triadic character.

The sight of nontriadic elements ("a roof, a gleam of sunlight reflected from a stone, the smell of a road") also gives him "a special pleasure" and they "appear to be concealing something";[5] and he eventually explains this pleasure (and, presumably—by implication—the hidden meaning) in terms of the superposition of past and present perceptions, giving an impression of sudden escape from time and mortality.[6] This, however, is a retrospective explanation, and while it explains the pleasure (and mystery) associated with the *recurrence* of the impression, it cannot suffice to explain the pleasure and mystery associated with the *first* perception, the first of the two superposed moments. The true explanation here would appear to be found in the protagonist's pleasure-giving symbiotic relationship with phenomena, which he anthropomorphizes. I have dealt with this aspect elsewhere.

To return to the triads: Gilles Deleuze affirms that the meaning, the "hidden content," of the three bell-towers is the group of girls which the narrator at one point suggests they represent.[7] Our objections to such an interpretation are based on Deleuze's uncritical attitude to what he believes Proust to be saying, his neglect of the first-person point of view (which leads him to confuse Proust

himself with the fictional narrator), his consequent passive acceptance of what the narrator says, and his misreading of the
statements which are the object of his passive acceptance. Furthermore, no significance is attached by Deleuze to the triadic character
of the group of bell-towers; I propose to suggest that their triadic
character is not only significant but indeed their *most* significant
character.

There are other mentions of bell-towers in the *Recherche*,[8] but
they are used principally, like the reference to the towers of the
Trocadéro,[9] simply to introduce the theme of the illusion of
nearness. Only the bell-towers of Martinville and Vieuxvicq, which
form a *triad*, are associated with a mysterious pleasure and a hidden
meaning. As for trees, the narrator merely notes the striking contrast between the light and shadow which fall upon them,[10] for example, and even the most beautiful flowering trees, in which the
protagonist sees "foreign gods," "angels,"[11] merely symbolize
transcendence. Again, only the *triad* of trees seen near Balbec is
strangely and profoundly significant.

Judging by the treatment of the only other triad in the
Recherche,[12] we can say that every triad of objects the protagonist
encounters provokes the same reaction in him. Of the passages dealing with the triads we have indicated, that involving the bell-towers
is the most important, and its central significance in the *Recherche*
as a whole is indicated by the fact that it is his writing-up of the experience which he later sends to the *Figaro* for publication as an article.[13]

II   The Sight of Triads and the Mysterious Pleasure it Affords

When the narrator first evokes the bell-towers, he begins with a
notation of the special pleasure the protagonist derives from observing them: "At a bend in the road I experienced, suddenly, that
special pleasure, which bore no resemblance to any other, when I
caught sight of the twin steeples of Martinville, on which the setting
sun was playing, while the movement of the carriage and the wind-
ings of the road seemed to keep them continually changing their
position; and then of a third steeple, that of Vieuxvicq, which,
although separated from them by a hill and a valley, and rising from
rather higher ground in the distance, appeared none the less to be
standing by their side."[14] Five pages later, when he reflects upon
the pleasure of seeing once again the landscapes of his childhood,

the very first image that occurs to him consists of another group of
three objects similarly made up of a closely-knit couple and a third a
little further off: ". . . what I want to see again is the 'Guermantes
way' as I knew it, with the farm that stood a little apart from the
two neighbouring farms, pressed so close together, at the entrance
to the oak avenue".[15] On a third occasion, we have another evocation of the pleasure caused by the sight of a triad of objects: "We
came down towards Hudimesnil; suddenly I was overwhelmed with
that profound happiness which I had not often felt since Combray;
happiness analogous to that which had been given me by—among
other things—the steeples of Martinville. But this time it remained
incomplete. I had just seen, standing a little way back from the
steep ridge over which we were passing, three trees, probably mark-
ing the entrance to a shady avenue, which made a pattern at which
I was looking now not for the first time."[16]

In the case of the trees and the bell-towers, which are thus expressly linked by the narrator, we find great emphasis placed on the
feeling that the cause of the pleasure experienced remains a
mystery. He says of the bell-towers: "In ascertaining and noting the
shape of their spires, the changes of aspect, the sunny warmth of
their surfaces, I felt that I was not penetrating to the full depth of
my impression, that something more lay behind that mobility, that
luminosity, something which they seemed at once to contain and to
conceal."[17] Similarly, he declares concerning the three trees: "I
looked at the three trees; I could see them plainly, but my mind felt
that they were concealing something which it had not grasped, as
when things are placed out of our reach, so that our fingers, stretch-
ed out at arm's-length, can only touch for a moment their outer surface, and can take hold of nothing."[18] There is, however, an important difference compared with his experience of the bell-towers,
which he indicates in these words referring to the happiness experienced at seeing the trees: "But this time it [the happiness]
remained incomplete."[19] In what way was the experience of the
bell-towers more "complete"? Of that occasion, he writes:
"Presently their outlines and their sunlit surfaces, as though they
had been a sort of rind, were stripped apart; a little of what they
had concealed from me became apparent; an idea came into my
mind which had not existed for me a moment earlier, framed itself
in words in my head; and the pleasure with which the first sight of
them, just now, had filled me was so much enhanced that, over-

powered by a sort of intoxication, I could no longer think of anything else."[20]

There is a further difference, possibly the most significant of all: on the occasion of seeing the bell-towers, the protagonist takes a step further and writes down on a sheet of paper a description of the bell-towers as they appeared to him in the course of his trip toward and later away from them.[21] This literary transposition further "completes" the experience so satisfactorily that we are told: "I never thought again of this page, but at the moment when, on my corner of the box-seat, where the Doctor's coachman was in the habit of placing, in a hamper, the fowls which he had bought at Martinville market, I had finished writing it, I found such a sense of happiness, felt that it had so entirely *relieved* my mind of the obsession of the steeples, and of the mystery which they concealed, that, as though I myself were a hen and had just laid an egg, I began to sing at the top of my voice."[22] The word *débarrassé* (translated by Scott Moncrieff as "relieved" but more literally meaning "rid") is a surprising choice, and makes one wonder whether the youngster really did want to *master* the bell towers and their mysterious meaning or rather to *escape from* them—and it. The young writer clearly experiences a feeling of achievement and relief—but is this feeling produced by the solution of his problem (that is, revelation of the enigmatic meaning or message hidden in the bell-towers) or by the *illusion* of such a solution (leaving the original enigma unresolved)? To answer this question, we must look more closely at the nature and function of the literary transposition of such triads.

III   The Function of Art: Spiritual Equivalent but False "Solution"

Here is the passage in which the narrator purports to "explain" the hidden meaning of the scene of the bell-towers: "In short, in this case as in the other, whether objective impressions such as I had received from the spires of Martinville, or subjective memories like the unevenness of the two steps or the taste of the *madeleine*, I must try to interpret the sensations as the indications of corresponding *laws* and *ideas;* I must try to think, that is to say, *bring out* of the obscurity what I had felt, and *convert* it into a spiritual equivalent. Now this method, which seemed to me the only one, what was it other than to create a work of art?"[23] This "explanation" of the hidden meaning of the bell towers, based on the highly questionable equating of "bring out" (*faire sortir*) with

"convert" (*convertir*), is most unconvincing. Instead of penetrating
the phenomena observed, he merely transposes them. One has the
impression that he is right in sensing a hidden meaning; one does
not have the impression that he has discovered just what that
hidden meaning is. What are the "laws"[24] and "ideas" of which he
suggests these sensations are so many "signs" (and the literary
transposition merely gives the "signs" of these "signs")? This question, the essential one (as he appears to realize), remains un-
answered.

If we examine closely the passage in which the protagonist, when
young, wrote up his perception of the bell-towers, the role of
anthropomorphosis appears highly significant. It is first implied in
the words chosen to describe the appearance and movements of the
elements thus perceived in relation to their setting: ". . . springing
into position in front of them by a daring volt, a third, dilatory steeple, that of Vieuxvicq, was come to join them . . . Then the steeple
of Vieuxvicq withdrew, took its proper distance, and the steeples of
Martinville remained alone. . . . Its steeples and that of Vieuxvicq
waved once again, in token of farewell, their sun-bathed pinnacles."[25] Then the series of images used to enrich the original impression ("like birds," "like golden pivots," "like painted flowers,"
"[like] three maidens in a legend") ends in the anthropomorphosis
of the final comparison: "They made me think, too, of three
maidens in a legend, abandoned in a solitary place over which night
had begun to fall; and while we drew away from them at a gallop, I
could see them timidly seeking their way, and, after some awkward,
stumbling movements of their noble silhouettes, drawing close to
one another, slipping one behind another, showing nothing more,
now, against the still rosy sky than a single dusky form, charming
and resigned, and so vanishing in the night."[26] It is when he
achieves this anthropomorphosis of the three bell towers that he
feels fulfilled and relieved, happy.

In the older narrator's later literary transposition of the three
trees, we find that he omits the intermediate images and moves
directly to the anthropomorphosis:

And yet all the time they were coming towards me; perhaps some
fabulous apparition, a ring of witches or of norns who would propound their
oracles to me. I chose rather to believe that they were phantoms of the past,
dear companions of my childhood, vanished friends who recalled our common memories. Like ghosts they seemed to be appealing to me to take
them with me, to bring them back to life. In their simple, passionate

gesticulation I could discern the helpless anguish of a beloved person who has lost the power of speech, and feels that he will never be able to say to us what he wishes to say and we can never guess. . . . I watched the trees gradually withdraw, waving their despairing arms, seeming to say to me: "What you fail to learn from us today, you will never know. If you allow us to drop back into the hollow of this road from which we sought to raise ourselves up to you, a whole part of yourself which we were bringing to you will fall for ever into the abyss. . . . I was as wretched as though I had just lost a friend, had broken faith with the dead or had denied my God.[27]

The transformation of the observed reality can be seen as an approach to a hidden meaning only if that meaning is in fact not present in (or "behind") the phenomena themselves but actually hidden in the mind. Such a hypothesis finds support in the fact that the feeling of penetration to this real meaning is associated most closely with the most anthropomorphous—and therefore the most psychological, the most personal—of the comparisons used. It may well be that what is significant is not so much *the fact of* the literary transposition as *its nature*—that is, the tendency to anthropomorphosis which reveals the level at which the triad plays symbolically upon the protagonist's imagination.

Why should the elevation of such triads of inanimate objects to the level of human existence be critically relevant to the *real* "hidden meaning" referred to, which the protagonist gropes for, even fancies he discovers, but in actual fact never attains?

IV Theories, Laws, and Ideas: New Truths and Hidden Meanings

Modern family psychotherapy has established that binary or two-person relationships are always basically unstable, and that the "molecule" or smallest building block of any emotional system is the three-person grouping.[28] This triangle is characterized by constant interaction between its elements. Now if we apply this knowledge to the study of literature, we may postulate that the intersubjective triangle may be represented by any triad of objects, and that its internal motion may be represented by internal movement within the symbolic triad. Happiness experienced whenever a triad of objects is seen, especially when these are explicitly taken to symbolize a triad of human beings (through anthropomorphosis), suggests the relief provided by "triangling-in" a third party characteristic of a person involved in a two-person relationship, however satisfying. Both bell-towers and farms suggest, through their "two plus one" configuration, not only the confirmation of the satisfying but unstable symbiotic two-person relationship through the addition ("triangling-in") of a third person in a spectator role, but also, and more importantly, the possibility of either member of the couple moving to the spectator position for temporary relief. One such two-person relationship is the excessively symbiotic relationship which is a common cause of schizophrenia. Now, precisely such a relationship is portrayed in the *Recherche*, as we have already established. *Combray* begins with the evocation of the symbiotic relationship between the child (the narrator's younger self) and the mother. The symbolic relevance (reference) of the trio of bell-towers to the corresponding human interrelationship-system is emphasized by the inclusion of the various main thrusts of the latter, such as the fact that the emotional forces within a triangle are in constant motion (represented by the illusion of movement given to the bell-towers by the constantly changing view from the winding road) and that the function of the triangle is modified by the modification of the function of one person within the triangle (symbolized by the varying function of the Vieuxvicq bell-tower).

Only in the case of the three farms is there no anthropomorphosis, but the latter is replaced here by their association with his mother's kiss: immediately after evoking his mother's face bent over him "without scruple or reservation, unburdened by any liability save to myself," he evokes thc trio of farms, one slightly apart and the other two "pressed close against each other."[29] Two of the farms are thus nestled together like the child and his mother, while the third is present but a little farther off (like the child's father?). The transition from face to farms must seem abrupt and almost grotesque if we fail to make this association and realize that the landscape element provides an external, "objectified" representation of the child's basic human relations. This therefore supports our hypothesis concerning the meaning of the other triads. The continually changing relations within the triad may be seen in the movement from the symbiotic relationship between mother and child to the triad in which the child moves temporarily to the "outsider" position: "that old desire to rebel against an imaginary plot woven against me by my parents (who imagined that I would be forced to obey them)."[30]

The central theme of the work is time, as we are expressly told by the narrator.[31] How is this theme related to the hidden meaning of the bell-towers of Martinville? The narrator's answer lies in the extratemporal position adopted by rememberer, comparer, and describer (writer). Another clue is provided by the last page of the work, where people of advanced age are seen as "perched on giant stilts, sometimes taller than church spires":[32] here, in a comparison explicitly using the image of bell-towers, space occurs as a metaphor for time. Further answers may be seen in the relationship between time and movement. The bell-towers are shown not in static, eternally fixed and unchangeable relationship but in perpetual (if totally subjective and illusory) movement—and that in several different senses. They move in relationship to the observer's own movement, and these movements are dramatized and include the observer in their meaning; they are involved in movement to other planes of reality through metamorphosis (comparison and writing-up) and further in the restless passage from one metamorphosis to another, imposed not by the geographical displacement of the observer's body (viewpoint) but by the various transpositions imposed by the ceaseless efforts of the writer's mind. Finally, it is striking that *Combray*, the opening phase of a struggle against the passage of time, takes us from the unstable binary mother-son relationship[33] to the stable ternary system symbolized by the three bell-towers and the three farms. Life and time are thus stabilized, halted; hence the feeling of relief, achievement, happiness caused to the protagonist by the sight of the symbolic triangular system—especially as captured, as immobilized in the written description (*écriture*).

My conclusion is that Proust's fictional narrator is a schizophrenic who does not want to give up the pleasures of symbiosis which produce and perpetuate his condition. When, as protagonist, he is faced with triads, especially of vertical objects like bell-towers and trees, his manner of relating to reality leads him naturally to anthropomorphize them. This gives him pleasure in various ways: first, it reminds him of his pleasure-giving relationship with his mother (bell-towers, farms); second, it enables him to see in them an image of the "triangling-in" of a third party which can provide relief, if temporarily desired, from the symbiotic two-person relationship, which is necessarily unstable. The third source of pleasure is provided by the literary transposition of the triads: this enables him to trade a partial avowal of the truth (through anthropomorpous comparisons) for the right to claim that *all* the truth has been disclosed. "Writing-up" thus becomes a sort of alibi for the schizophrenic, who does not want to face the unpalatable truth that he really ought to free himself from the symbiosis which maintains him in his schizophrenic state.

If this hypothesis is valid, then previous critics appear to have imitated the Proustian narrator in skating over this "hidden meaning" without ever penetrating it: they have swallowed his literary alibi. We need to rethink both the meaning of these various triads and the function of their literary transposition, for these elements shed a precious and apparently neglected light on the psychological makeup of Proust's fictional narrator, and consequently on the deep structure of the work as a whole.

CHAPTER 7

Patterns

THE basic shaping pattern of the *Recherche* is provided
by the antithesis between the real and the ideal, expressed
most commonly through the opposition Méséglise/Guermantes but
also through the polarity Combray/Venice. There are two fundamental structuring principles, the one linear and the other circular. The linear one, marked by the movement from idealism
(Guermantes' way) to realism (Swann's way) and from life to death,
is essentially pessimistic, as reflected in the deaths of Albertine and
Robert, the degeneration of Charlus and Saint-Loup, the triumph of
the pretentious and sadistic Mme. Verdurin, and the impoverish-
ment of the protagonist. The circular structure, on the other hand,
moves from idealism to realism and back to idealism—from time
possessed to time lost to time recovered, from the idealism of inex-
perience to the realism of experience and back to the idealism of
literary creation; it may not implausibly be interpreted as a structure of compensation.

The same antithesis also finds expression through color symbolism, directly indicated at certain points,[1] in which the
"idealistic" blondness of the Guermantes, manifested notably in
Oriane and even more in Saint-Loup, is opposed to the "realistic"
darkness of Morel and Albertine. Between the yellow or gold which
symbolizes Oriane and the black which symbolizes Albertine is the
intermediate color of mauve or violet (described as "washed out"
and "dissolute") associated with Odette through Vinteuil's little
phrase (it evokes "the mauve tumult of the sea"), her favorite
flowers, and her clothes. Even morally there seems to be a symbolic
relationship between the "dissolute colour" of the Parma violets
and the somewhat anaemic type of beauty possessed by Odette.
Because of this association, Odette comes immediately to mind
when Oriane snobbishly says of some mauve flowers that "as it can
happen with people who are very pretty and very well dressed, they
have an ugly name and smell bad."[2]

The work is quite exceptionally rich in symbolic and archetypal dimensions. Even the world of Greek mythology, with its coded archetypal patterns, is exploited at times, as in the passage on perfumes. Of these references, however, many, such as those to Hercules, are of little more interest than the empty rhetorical effusions and pseudoclassical elucubrations of Bloch. Perhaps the figure of Orpheus may be excepted because of its singular appropriateness to the narrator's concern with death, lost love, and artistic creation. Other sources of myth and legend are also exploited to provide such figures as the fairy Mélusine, whose fate was so intimately related to that of the illustrious Lusignan family; the fairy is identified with the magic hidden in a legendary name, and thus constitutes a privileged symbol of metamorphosis and the fragile transcendence of ordinary reality. But the archetypal dimension is mostly expressed otherwise—through the treatment of certain objects, whether natural (flowers, the moon, the sea) or man-made (clothes, windows, bells, steeples); the manner of depicting actions, like eating or kissing, or profound and universal relationships—with father, mother, or the opposite sex; and references to archetypal patterns such as the Quest or the Orphic Descent.

I   *The Window as Symbolic Threshold to Transcendence*

The general relationship between the object and what it symbolizes, between the real and the imaginary, the material and the spiritual, the profane and the sacred is represented in some literary works (for example, *The Red and the Black*) by the symbol of the bird, which belongs to the earth through its animal nature but transcends it by flight. In the *Recherche*, the symbol used most frequently is that of the window, rich in implications both of the relationship and of the separation of the here-and-now and the beyond. The window is barrier, limit, pseudothreshold, but also viewpoint, revelation, participation. Although it occurs much less frequently than in, say, *Madame Bovary* (where it represents a yearning for a better fate which passes from Charles dreaming of the country to Emma dreaming of the city), it is used with a rich and effective elaboration in the *Recherche*. In fact, it (or a substitute—stained-glass windows, magic lantern) appears at the beginning or end of several sections of the work, thus constituting a thematic symbol with a central structuring function. Aunt Léonie's whole view of life is structured by the frame of her window, and this role of spectator is often given to a person who dominates at the given moment.

When the protagonist first sees Gilberte, the narrator writes: "I gazed at her, at first with that gaze which is not merely a messenger from the eyes, but in whose window all the senses assemble and lean out, petrified and anxious, that gaze which would fain reach, touch, capture, bear off in triumph the body at which it is aimed, and the soul with the body."[3] This conception of his own gaze as intimate, urgent person-to-person contact may be transferred to another's somewhat different gaze which is not so much communication as spectacle—the window metaphor again being used: the group of male admirers which framed Odette "gave to this woman, in whose eyes alone was there any intensity, the air of looking out in front of her, from among all those men, as from a window from behind which she had taken her stand, and made her emerge there, frail but fearless, in the nudity of her delicate colours, like the apparition of a creature of a different species, of an unknown race, and of almost martial strength, by virtue of which she seemed by herself a match for all her multiple escort."[4]

The window image may represent a transposition from one sense to another, as from sound to sight, as in the affirmation of the transparency of the interpretation of great music by a great pianist ("he is nothing now but a window opening upon a great work of art")[5] or in the visual connotations of the first warble of pigeons: "Meanwhile the winter was drawing to an end. One morning, after several weeks of showers and storms, I heard in my chimney—instead of the wind, formless, elastic, sombre, which convulsed me with a longing to go to the sea—the cooing of the pigeons that were nesting in the wall outside; shimmering, unexpected, like a first hyacinth, gently tearing open its fostering heart that there might shoot forth, purple and satin-soft, its flower of sound, letting in like an opened window into my bedroom still shuttered and dark the heat, the dazzling brightness, the fatigue of a first fine day."[6] The window (not as metaphor this time but as literal object) may give a view upon a dramatic and beautiful reality, such as that of the snowy-crested, deep emerald waves of the open sea.

Sometimes the relationship between the symbol of the window and the theme of the sacred (that is, of transcendence) is explicitly stated: the outlook from the end of the corridor of the protagonist's floor of the hotel at Balbec exposes to his "adoration" a distant view of a solitary mansion resembling "one of those architectural works in miniature, tiny temples or chapels wrought in gold and enamels, which serve as reliquaries and are exposed only on rare and solemn days for the veneration of the faithful."[7] The mysterious beauty perceived through a window may of course be a woman: "Looking away up, one could make out in the dim, golden-yellow light, a woman who, in this engulfing darkness in which she seemed like an anchorite, took on the veiled, mysterious charm of a vision of the Orient."[8]

The window has a feminine connotation not only through its association with Odette, Albertine, and the sea but also through its function of receiving and being entered and traversed by the glance or gaze. The feminine character of this universe as a whole is suggested by the presence of several such symbols, another of which is the bell, to which we shall return shortly.

II   *Sacred Time, the Sound of Bells, and the Kiss of Death*

The association of sleep with the sacred is an important theme at the beginning of the work: "When a man is asleep, he has in a circle round him the chain of the hours, the sequence of the years, the order of the heavenly host."[9] The key phrase "in a circle" stresses the difference between sacred time, which is cyclical and therefore eternal, and profane time, which is linear and terminal. Sacred time reappears frequently in the course of the *Recherche*—the seasonal variations in weather, the concomitant life-style (city versus country or seaside), and above all the flowers, all of which have a cyclical rhythm and can therefore be counted on to reappear in future years in endless incarnations. The flowers, especially, recall—almost embody—the ever-changing but never-ending cycle of the religious calendar year, and the language in which they are described explicitly conjures up the sacred which hovers like an aura behind profane reality.

The narrator remarks that "holy days stood out more clearly at the end of those that merely came between,"[10] and there are numerous references to religious ceremonial. The servants' meal is a "solemn passover" with Françoise, "who was at one and the same time, as in the primitive church, the celebrant and one of the faithful";[11] the cider and cherries eaten for supper are viewed as "'kinds' in which I should have made the most perfect communion."[12] The *salon* of the Guermantes is as sacred and mysterious

as the Holy Eucharist, its guests are like the sacred columns or
statues of this temple, the friendship of the Duchesse is like a divine
presence, and her life is an inaccessible Paradise. The Guermantes'
dinner guests "assembled there indeed, like the early Christians,
. . . in a sort of social Eucharist."[13] There is even something "sacer-
dotal" in Aimé's manner of carving the young turkeys.

The notion that circular time, not only that of the calendar but
that of the day with its eternally renewed waxing and waning, is
linked to the sacred is strikingly emphasized in the following
dramatic passage: "I could not repress a sob when, with a gesture of
oblation mechanically performed which appeared to me to symbolize the bloody sacrifice which I should have to make of all joy,
every morning, until the end of my life, a solemn renewal,
celebrated as each day dawned, of my daily grief and of the blood
from my wound, the golden egg of the sun, as though propelled by
the breach of equilibrium brought about at the moment of coagula-
tion by a change of density, barbed with tongues of flame as in a
painting, came leaping through the curtain behind which one had
felt that it was quivering with impatience, ready to appear on the
scene and to spring aloft, the mysterious, ingrained purple of which
it flooded with waves of light."[14]

The sacred finds a more profound expression in deeper and more
sincere human relations, such as those which unite the narrator's
mother and grandmother: he describes his mother as offering to her
mother the whole of her life in her face as in a ciborium. Swann sees
in Odette's lies a sacred veil hiding an infinitely precious reality; the
narrator sees in a waiter a young god running; and the death of love
lends a touch of the sacred to even the basest of rituals, as we are
told of Vinteuil's daughter, whose sacrilege toward her father was
founded on her adoration of him. It may also be seen in aspects of
nature, such as the rugged holy-water stoup of the oyster and the
huge white monstrances of the flowering fruit trees: the latter evoke
strange, poetic, ephemeral, local celebrations and especially a first
communion day.

A familiar symbol of the sacred is the bell, whose traditional symbolism here takes several forms: it represents wisdom (as opposed to
method) and the passive, feminine principle (as opposed to the active, male principle, represented by lightning); it suggests, by the
rapid extinction of the sound, the shallow and fading world of
appearances; and it warns of the approach of evil influences, may
ward them off, even exorcise and purify. In the *Recherche*, the

sound of a bell may be a sign and a signal of servitude ("our young master's wretched bell") or of the rhythms of country life, as the bugle's fanfare is of military life. The bell's ringing is also translated into other sensations: its sound is golden, like honey, and full of light; hovering over the set dining-table like a wasp, it takes on the flavors of the food; the modifications it experiences as the weather changes make of it a musical translation of the sunshine or the rain. The sound of bells is incorporated by Vinteuil into his Septuor, in a passage which at first displeases the protagonist but later becomes the part he prefers.

Bells precede various types of eclipse of healthy life—sickness and death, and above all the kiss which is followed by sleep. A veritable gamut of bells large and small—*cloches, clochettes, sonnettes, grelots*—punctuates the evocation of the ritual exchange of kisses which permits access to the realm of sleep. The periodic and detested interdiction of the rite is signaled by the sound of a bell: "not the large and noisy rattle which heralded and deafened as he approached with its ferruginous, interminable, frozen sound any member of the household who set it off by coming in 'without ringing,' but the double peal—timid, oval, gilded—of the visitors' bell."[15] The departure of the intruder is announced by the sound of the *grelot:* "the reverberating, ferruginous, interminable, sharp, jangling tinkle of the little bell."[16] The profound significance of this little sound is affirmed in the very last pages of the *Recherche.* The interdiction is confirmed by the dinner bell, signal at which his father sends him up to bed without his good-night kiss.

The little boy's love for his mother is manifested and symbolized especially in the good-night kiss. When this kiss has to be given hastily in public, he determines to make the most of this kiss which must be so short and furtive, carefully choosing the place on her cheek which he would kiss, preparing himself mentally to extract the absolute maximum of pleasure from the time allowed for kissing her. The exchanging of the kiss is referred to as "these rites," her face as "a host for a communion of peace," and as a "viaticum" this precious kiss which his mother gave him at the moment of his going to sleep.

His mother's kiss is not the only one which is linked to the sacred; he writes of Albertine: "Late every night, before leaving me, she used to slide her tongue between my lips like a portion of daily bread, a nourishing food that had the almost sacred character of all flesh upon which the sufferings that we have endured on its account

have come in time to confer a sort of spiritual grace."[17] The analogy
with the swallowing of the communion is made more vivid by the
replacement of the mother's face by Albertine's tongue.

The Holy Communion thus symbolized by the kiss is also evoked
by the transcendence of immediate reality through the partaking of
a cake (the *madeleine*) soaked in tea. The ritual character of kissing
may, of course, be emphasized or minimized. It is minimal in the
charming page evoking the endless kisses showered on Odette by
Swann and in some of the passages where Albertine kisses the
protagonist. In other passages the act of kissing is charged with
significance without ritualization—these are passages where the
anthropophagous character of the act is emphasized.[18] The magnificent, almost naked breasts of Mme de Surgis fascinate and in-
toxicate Swann, and the narrator remarks that it becomes impossible
to resist kissing a bare shoulder one has gazed at too long. The same
lady's suspicions with regard to Charlus' chin-pinching tendencies
are expressly linked to fears of cannibalism,[19] and the protagonist's
fixation on cheeks appears to partake of the same character.[20] Before
the first page of the *Recherche* is over, he has evoked this penchant:
"I would lay my cheeks gently against the comfortable cheeks of my
pillow, as plump and blooming as the cheeks of babyhood."[21] His
need to kiss his mother is a need to kiss her cheek (substitute, no
doubt, for the oral pleasure associated with the maternal
breast[22]—the cheeks he prefers are always pink, round, full)—"look
out very carefully first the exact spot on her cheek where I would
imprint the kiss, and so prepare my thoughts as to be able, thanks to
these mental preliminaries, to consecrate the whole of the minute
Mamma would allow me to the sensation of her cheek against my
lips."[23]

He finds one girl's cheeks so pretty that they intimidate him, and
to kiss Albertine is to know at last the taste of her cheeks. Albertine's laughter evokes the *inside* of her cheeks(!)—"the rosy flesh,
the fragrant portals between which it has just made its way."[24] He
speaks of "the charming pink globe of her cheeks" and of "the taste
of this fleshly rose," and laments that "the lips, designed to convey
to the palate the taste of whatever whets the appetite, must be content, without ever realizing their mistake or admitting their disappointment, with roaming over the surface and with coming to a halt
at the barrier of the impenetrable but irresistible cheek."[25] This
desire for penetration is satisfied by the replacement of the cheek as
object by the mouth: "She passed her tongue lightly over my lips

which she attempted to force apart";[26] "I could feel, against my lips which she was trying to part, her tongue, her motherly, inedible, nourishing and holy tongue whose secret flame and dew meant that even when Albertine let it glide over the surface of my throat or stomach, those caresses, superficial but in a sense offered by her inmost flesh, turned outward like a cloth that is turned to show its lining, assumed even in the most external touches as it were the mysterious delight of a penetration."[27]

Finally, the kiss of life (of Creator to creature) and the kiss of death (of Judas to Christ) are strikingly combined in the kiss exchanged between the protagonist and his mother. While his mother, to whom he owed the original gift of life, gives him a life-giving kiss (without it, he does not want to live any longer), the kiss he gives her in return will ultimately bring about her death, as we saw earlier.[28]

191053

III *Woman as Mother, Mistress, Queen, Priestess, Goddess*

Woman occupies a central position in the *Recherche*, and fills many different but interrelated roles. She is a mother, and as such the object of deep love and need or of painful neglect; capable of bringing relief and calm (as other women will later), she is more usually a source of pain deriving from "this terrible need for a person."[29] The central importance of the relationship between the protagonist and his mother has already been explored. The role of the mother figure is further enhanced by reference to other mothers—those of Gilberte, of Andrée, and (by "adoption") of Albertine. A curious link between parent figures—the mother of Gilberte and the mother figure of Albertine, the father of Mlle Vinteuil—is their representation in painting or photograph, which lends itself to the ritualization of their role and, in the Vinteuil case, to ritual profanation.

The legendary hero Golo—whose introduction in the very first pages suggests the epic character of the quest (*Recherche*) being undertaken—is, as we have mentioned already, one of the many surrogates for the protagonist. This is dramatically revealed in the following passage: "I would run down to . . . fall into the arms of my mother, whom the misfortunes of Geneviève de Brabant made all the dearer to me, just as the crimes of Golo had driven me to a more than ordinarily scrupulous examination of my own conscience."[30] Here we have a remarkable evocation of the intense relationship with the mother; and its depiction is frequently accompanied by evocations of the father, who is shown as annoyed at the mother's concessions to the little boy and as ridiculing his desire to spend a long time kissing her good-night. The gravity of the matter is strongly emphasized: the protagonist is convinced that by staying up to kiss his mother good-night as she came up to bed he runs the serious risk of being packed off to a boarding-school the next day. Yet his audacity is not punished but rewarded: his mother, at the suggestion of his father, spends the night in his room.

She is mistress, and the message repeated over and over again by the narrator is that, in spite of minor differences, the women in one man's life (in his case, Gilberte, Mme de Guermantes, Albertine) are virtually interchangeable. Besides these realistic functions, woman may be seen as a transcendent creature—queen, priestess, goddess. Odette's intimate association with the sacred is suggested several times, through two levels of transformation: that of royalty and that of divinity. Her assimilation to royalty, which depends partly on her relationship with Swann, is suggested by the use of terms like "kingdom," "palace," "throne," and "crowned heads." But stronger terms, with a religious connotation, like "sanctuary," are also used. In a particularly notable passage, the narrator declares that "being assured in my own mind that, in accordance with the liturgy, with the ritual in which Mme Swann was so profoundly versed, her clothes were connected with the time of year and of day by a bond both inevitable and unique, I felt that the flowers upon the stiff straw brim of her hat, the baby-ribbons upon her dress had been even more naturally born of the month of May than the flowers in gardens and in woods; and to learn what latest change there was in weather or season I had not to raise my eyes higher than to her parasol, open and outstretched like another, a nearer sky, round, clement, mobile, blue."[31] A little later, she is described as conforming her choice of clothes to the season "as though yielding to a superior wisdom of which she herself was high priestess." She is evoked "behind the most brilliant 'turn-out,' the smartest liveries in Paris, gently and majestically seated, like a goddess."

Oriane has a personal charm that made her fashionable and "something of a queen";[32] Rachel is clothed by Saint-Loup in an almost religious mystery;[33] Mme de Cambremer wears "the ornaments of her pastoral visitation and her social priesthood."[34] The narrator sees goddesses in the objects of his desire—first in society women, later in working girls. Albertine is "a many-headed goddess," "a great goddess of Time."[35] Mme Verdurin, preoccupied with "her little Church," is a "deity presiding over musical rites, patron saint of Wagnerism and sick-headaches, a sort of almost tragic norn".[36] Among images of this type, the only dramatic one is that describing the bloodletting of his grandmother: "The tiny black serpents were writhing among her blood-stained locks, as on the head of Medusa."[37]

The relationship between woman and the sacred is evoked by the comparison between women (Odette, Albertine) and the moon, traditionally seen as an embodiment of the female principle because of its monthly cycle and its sway over the watery element: "As the moon, which is no more than a tiny white cloud of a more definite and fixed shape than other clouds during the day, assumes her full power as soon as daylight dies, so when I was once more in the hotel it was Albertine's sole image that rose from my heart and began to shine."[38]

Another symbol combines the eternal feminine with the notion of mortality: it is the *madeleine*, whose shell-like design links it with shell symbolism in general, which is very rich, involving water, fertility, the female sexual organ (Aphrodite, the pearl in the shell), good luck, the moon, the womb. The prosperity it symbolizes is however one which depends on death (that of the previous occupant of the shell)—theme of the endless come and go of the successive generations; birth, life, birth. Rebirth is symbolized in the association of shell forms with the rite of baptism.

IV *Eros, Thanatos, and the Return to the Womb*

The power of Eros is represented at times, as when it makes death appear indifferent or even impossible;[39] but it is Thanatos that predominates. The work opens in an atmosphere of stillness, darkness, and silence—the manifestations of the inanimate, of Thanatos.[40] Gradually there is a movement from night to day, from the one to the many, from interior to exterior, the latter taking the form of an expulsion from the womb. A rich ambiguity, however, overlays these structures and forestalls facile interpretations. If the movements I have just evoked are negative—and there are several suggestions that to travel is to be ill and to yearn for a return to the womb[41]—nevertheless the womb is a place of privation, of separation from the mother. Consequently, the womb-bedroom is seen as

a grave,[42] and the staircase leading up to it as a vehicle of transcendence over sensuality (the mother's kiss) which excites only
resentment and hatred.

Sometimes, the death wish (Thanatos) is motivated by self-
respect (and is therefore false) but nevertheless striking: "Thus I
find myself, albeit the least courageous of men, to have known that
feeling which has always seemed to me, in my reasoning moods, so
foreign to my nature, so inconceivable, the intoxication of danger.
But even although I were, when any, even a deadly peril threatened
me, passing through an entirely calm and happy phase, I could not,
were I with another person, refrain from sheltering him behind me
and choosing for myself the post of danger."[43] At other times,
however, on more specific occasions, the negative desire is both explicit and authentic: "Having no world, no room, no body now that
was not menaced by the enemies thronging round me, invaded to
the very bones by fever, I was utterly alone; I longed to die."[44]

The narrator clearly implies that the love of life is foreign to him,
referring to "the love of life and the love of fame, since there are, it
appears, persons who are acquainted with these latter sentiments."[45]

There are several further ways in which the principle of Thanatos
is manifested in the *Recherche*. Thus, to equate love with jealousy
and pain is to condemn Eros, and to yearn to eliminate time and
temporality is to long for the abolition of movement and animation.
The valorization of silence and stillness,[46] the suppression of sound,
represent a suppression of life and a descent into a strange and un-
recognizable universe.[47] The abandonment to fatigue and deep
sleep likewise constitutes a sort of Orphic Descent,[48] and even more
so the experience of death (of the Other) prefigured by the
telephone's suppression of corporal presence: "Over and again, as I
listened in this way, without seeing her who spoke to me from so far
away, it has seemed to me that the voice was crying to me from
depths out of which one does not rise again, and I have known the
anxiety that was one day to wring my heart when a voice should
thus return (alone, and attached no longer to a body which I was
never more to see), to murmur, in my ear, words I would fain have
kissed as they issued from lips for ever turned to dust."[49]

This interpretation is confirmed by the early introduction of the
notion of sickness,[50] associated with darkness and silence[51] and with
spatial restriction,[52] and by the association of sickness with travel.[53]
The archetype of the infirm traveler is a familiar one, embodied in
such figures as the blind seer Tiresias or the self-blinded Oedipus; it

suggests the sacred wounding or mutilation inflicted on the initiate, the seer, or the poet. The narrator's comparison of himself with Dante reinforces the notion of initiation, for Dante described himself as being initiated by Virgil through his journeys in the *Divina Commedia*.

The narrator refuses to avoid the pain and suffering caused by his jealousy, for "it is grief that develops the powers of the mind"; but this refusal is death-oriented, as he admits: "In the end, sorrow kills."[54] He is finally quite conscious of the probable result of his point of view: "The idea of suffering as an ineluctable prerequisite has become associated in our minds with the idea of work; we dread each new undertaking because of the suffering we know we must first go through to formulate it in our imagination. And when we understand that suffering is the best thing we can encounter in life, we contemplate death without dismay as a sort of emancipation."[55]

The passage where Albertine reveals (or claims) a close relationship with Mlle Vinteuil is followed by a remarkable page revealing an obscure but powerful guilt complex on the part of the protagonist,[56] concerning his apparently accidental but voyeuristic observation of a scene of lesbianism many years earlier.[57] He says of that occasion: "I had perilously allowed to expand within myself the fatal road, destined to cause me suffering, of Knowledge. And at the same time, from my bitterest grief I derived a sentiment almost of pride, almost joyful, that of a man whom the shock he has just received has carried at a bound to a point to which no voluntary effort could have brought him."[58] This development seems to represent for the protagonist a kind of Orphic Descent, perilous and frightening because of the broken taboo but also intoxicating in its promise of deep and ancient knowledge to be won. The notion of *transgression* is paramount here.

The notion of *Bildung* or maturation is raised to the level of ritual initiation by several textual indications. In heavy sleep, says the narrator, his mind lost all consciousness of the place in which he had fallen asleep, and when he awoke in the middle of the night he had no more consciousness of his existence than an animal or a caveman.[59] The subsequent initiation takes the form (discernible also in *Manon Lescaut* and above all in *Germinal*) of an adventure in a labyrinth. This notion is suggested at the end of walks around Combray (as by later passages on Paris and Venice): his father would take the family through unfamiliar and bewildering streets, and when they all felt completely lost he would point out the little back gate of their own garden, to which he had brought them back without their realizing it.[60] Thus the father alone has the key to the labyrinth of streets, paths, and walks around Combray, which play a significant role in the protagonist's maturation. The theme reappears later (with less emphasis) in association with Andrée, likened implicitly to Ariadne.[61]

Upon the triadic psychological core of its foundations, which is in itself essentially symbolic in nature, the *Recherche* builds a dialectical structure centered on geographical and color symbols. This in turn is clothed in a rich pattern of elements—windows, flowers, bells, meals, kisses—so treated as to exploit their potential as universal symbols, or archetypes. Of the categories of character similarly treated, woman plays the most remarkable role, often transformed by association with the sacred. However, she is less Aphrodite, the eternal Mistress, than the Mother, symbol of birth and therefore of death, of mortality: the *Recherche*, in its darkling shroud of sickness, neurosis, painful jealousy, unbearable guilt feelings, and ever-threatening despair, expresses not Eros but Thanatos, principle of stasis and silence, of sleep and death, of the inanimate state in which all at last is One forever. It is this longed-for nothingness which awaits the protagonist upon his finding his way at last through the labyrinth of Combray.

CHAPTER 8

Memories

I   *Tea-Cakes and Paving-Stones*

WHILE the past (for example, childhood years in Combray) may be called up by a position adopted while lying in bed, its most dramatic evocation appears unquestionably to be that provoked by the reliving of a more sensual and pleasurable, a more symbolic experience, as demonstrated by the effect of tasting the little cake soaked in lime tea. The passage evoking this experience closes section 1 of *Combray* (thus providing, with the first six pages, a circular framework for the longer central section) and also acts as a further stepping-stone through the gilded waters of the past; for just as Combray "emerged, town and gardens, from (his) cup of tea," so section 2, which follows and develops out of this episode of the tea-soaked cake, begins with the word "Combray" and is devoted to the evocation of the little town. (This evocation further contains within itself the original episode of the *madeleine,* whose recurrence triggers off the evocation.) And the same section two is rounded off with a further reference to the "old days at Combray . . . the memory of which has been more lately restored to me by the taste . . . of a cup of tea."[1]

A similar type of experience occurs again within *Combray,* this time provoked by the view of "some belfry of a hospital, or a convent steeple lifting the peak of its ecclesiastical cap at the corner of the street";[2] the difference is that this time the experience of "a tract of land reclaimed from oblivion" appears to be explained immediately or even beforehand, in the vague perception of resemblance: "my memory need only find in it some dim resemblance to that dear vanished outline." Although one does wonder whether there is more when one reads the suggestive and enigmatic "open" ending of the passage: "I am still seeking my way, I turn a corner . . . but . . . it is in my heart . . ."

In *The Past Recaptured* (*Le Temps retrouvé*), which closes the entire *Recherche* (the quest thus being declared successful), we find a summary of the whole work and a theoretical explanation. At the beginning of this passage, phenomena causing a strange joy and involving involuntary memory and also other phenomena causing the same reaction but not involving memory are grouped together and treated similarly: "In recovering my balance, I put my foot on a stone that was a little lower than the one next to it; immediately all my discouragement vanished before a feeling of happiness which I had experienced at different moments of my life, at the sight of trees I thought I recognized when driving around Balbec, or the church spires of Martinville, or the savour of a *madeleine* dipped in herb tea, or from many other sensations I have mentioned."[3] Later, however, the latter (phenomena not involving memory), which are visual and involve new truths, are distinguished from the former, which are more physical and involve remembered sensations.[4]

The protagonist perceives the feeling of happiness released in him by the sensations caused by uneven paving-stones, the sound of a spoon striking a plate, the feeling of a starched napkin, the noise of a water pipe.[5] He notes the identity between this happiness and that caused earlier by the taste of the tea-cake soaked in lime tea, and that the paving-stones, napkin, and tea-cake evoked Venice, Balbec, and Combray respectively. He develops the idea that such sensations cause happiness by relating the present to the past in a transient identity of two moments and two places, so that the passage of time between the two linked occurrences is abolished and the person experiencing the identification finds himself transported out of time and beyond its servitude. This experience of extratemporality brings with it a joy deriving from liberation from mortality—from the fear of death—through transfer to an ideal, Platonic level of existence, or rather, of essences. The protagonist feels solicited by such experiences, although he is not sure in what sense; ultimately he declares that the answer is to be found in the fixing or immortalizing of this transient joy and equanimity (and even of the essence of these sensations, from which the joy derives) through the transmutation of art.

In the course of this theoretical discussion, the narrator comes out strongly for connotation as against denotation, against discursive intelligence. In a significant footnote, he speaks of the relationship between names and words, images and ideas. Great emphasis is placed on impressions made by external reality: "Art is the most real of all things, the sternest school in Life and truly the Last Judgment. This book, the most difficult of all to decipher, is also the only one dictated to us by reality, the only one the 'imprinting' of which on our consciousness was done by reality itself. No matter what idea life may have implanted within us, its material representation, the outline of the impression it has made upon us, is always the guarantee of its indispensable truth. The ideas formed by pure intellect have only a logical truth, a potential truth; the selection of them is an arbitrary act. The book written in symbolic characters not traced by us is our only book."[6]

II *Time, Habit, and Memory*

The overall title states that the search for lost time is the goal of the protagonist; the title of the last book—*The Past Recaptured (Le Temps retrouvé)*—suggests that this search has been successful. The first word is "Longtemps" (translated as "For a long time"), the last is "le Temps." The narrator studies the instant, movement, and sentimental as distinct from chronological time.

Man is subject to the limitations imposed by time, and the narrator associates this inescapable tyranny with his own father: the latter, by declaring that the protagonist's tastes will not change any further, cuts the umbilical cord which keeps him in a sustaining dependence and thrusts him out into the throes of an autonomous existence, and subject to the laws of passing time.[7] Whereas his father, by embedding him at last in time, has deprived him of his illusion of immortality, Albertine, on the contrary, will appear to him as a benevolent fairy *(magicienne)*, providing him with a mirror of time—she so thoroughly embodies Balbec and the springtime season of the year that she restores to him his past, which thus comes to fill the painful gap left by his amputated future.[8] This restoration is of course based on seasonal circularity, and thus if his father stands for linear (or profane) time, Albertine stands for circular (or sacred) time. Seasonal or sacred time is also represented by several delightful evocations of Odette and her toilettes, which harmonize quite deliberately and perfectly with the changing seasons, and in the street cries of the various vendors and pedlars.[9]

Besides this means of actually escaping from linear time, life has a means of dulling our sense of its passage: this means is provided by habit. The narrator dwells at length on the phenomenon of habit, whose importance he often emphasizes with an initial capital letter. He sees it as ubiquitous, speaks of "the immense strength of Habit," and remarks that in love it is easier to give up a feeling than to lose a habit. Daily life is weighed down in banality by the balast of habit, and when we wish to avoid painful thoughts we call on the aid of habit. But habit is a mixed blessing. It does reconcile to the new and strange, and efface memory (the narrator speaks of "habit's eraser"), but this effacement, while it has a positive side (dulling the pain of separation, for example), is also a sort of death of our self. Consequently, the effort not to forget is a form of resistance to death. Habit paralyzes the imagination, and the narrator remarks: "If there were no such thing as habit, life must appear delightful to those of us who would at every moment be threatened with death—that is to say, to all mankind."[10] When traveling in a train, the protagonist is freed from the blindness and dulled faculties caused by routine and habit: "My habits, which were sedentary and were not matutinal, played me false, and all my faculties came hurrying to take their place, vieing with one another in their zeal."[11] Elsewhere, the word will occur five times in seven lines, all with capital letters, in a passage emphasizing the paradoxical (because extremely complex) character of the laws which govern the functioning of habit.

The positive value of habit is accompanied by a negative side which is sometimes indicated, namely the suppression of any feeling of reality as immediate, new, and full of revelations. But its positive side can provide solace against the painful contact with the unfamiliar, seen as indifferent or even hostile. Elsewhere, also, reference is made to other "selves" of earlier years which had been effaced by habit but return when habit is broken. Habit is a veil which must be broken through but the breaking with habit may prove an excruciatingly painful experience. Aunt Léonie leads a life entirely devoted to the observation of certain habits and customs which have gradually acquired the status of ritual. Within this sacred cycle, minor deviations, if constantly repeated, do not so much disturb the routine as they confirm it: such is the family's tradition of lunching an hour earlier on Saturdays. The cause of it is profane, being constituted by Françoise's departure after lunch for the market at Roussainville-le-Pin, but this profane character is totally transformed by ritualization and sacralization. This *regularized* deviation is as much of a change from (or rather, of course, within) the weekly routine as Aunt Léonie can bear. And the protagonist himself when a child cherished the moment when, upon returning from a walk in which he had become quite disoriented, he saw again the familiar garden gate and could abandon himself to the consoling care of habit, which would lead him to his room and lay him down to rest.

Profane time brings with it such phenomena as memory, temporal distanciation, and what are termed "the intermittences of the heart," somewhat analogous to visual saturation. The passage from sacred time, in which the Self is as if dissolved into an eternal stream of time, to profane time, which restores the separate identity of everyday life, is attributed to memory. In the young, memory is overwhelmed by the vivacity of present sensations and sentiments. Temporal distanciation results in a form of idealization. Time uses the intermittence of memory to release us momentarily from painful situations, as in the case of Swann's father who is distracted from the sorrow of his wife's death by the sunshine in the park, the breeze, the hawthorns, and the pond. Does the presence of the Other become a burden with the years? It is true that Aunt Léonie's worst nightmare is that her husband Octave had come back to life.

The theme of time—time past and time passing—is of course intimately related to that of memory and its opposite, forgetfulness. One kind of forgetfulness (inattention) can protect us against another: "What a person recalls to us most vividly is precisely what we had forgotten, because it was of no importance, and had therefore been left in full possession of its strength. That is why the better part of our memory is . . . hidden from our eyes, in an oblivion more or less prolonged. It is thanks to this oblivion alone that we can from time to time recover the creature that we were. . . . In the broad daylight of our ordinary memory the images of the past turn gradually pale and fade out of sight, nothing remains of them, we shall never find them again."[12]

III   *Love and Music*

As I pointed out earlier, the psychology proposed to us by the narrator is essentially a psychology of immaturity, and the laws and principles he proposes as *generally* valid are in fact, on the contrary, valid only for the immature and for a relatively small number of pathological cases. Is the protagonist's attitude toward Albertine (like that of Swann toward Odette) essentially one of jealousy or one of sadism—and concomitant masochism? It appears to be linked with the general tendency on the part of the protagonist to relate

sadistically to the loved and idealized woman in his life, including
his mother, his grandmother, and Françoise.

It is the linear dimension of time which explains the pain of
frustrated desire, as in the episode in which Swann's visit is to prevent the protagonist's mother from visiting him to give him his
good-night kiss, and the loss of love, as in the evocation of the
young woman who has come "to bury herself" in the country near
Combray in order to flee, perhaps hoping to forget, a lost love. Love
is further bound to time by its association with the symbol of music,
a link that is evoked indirectly in a reference to the flies executing
their little concert of summer chamber music. Musical airs are
presented as intoxicating but cruel, pitiless as the Eternal Feminine,
"because any such thing as a disinterested feeling for beauty, a
gleam of intelligence was unknown to them; for them physical
pleasures alone existed."[13]

A famous motif is "Vinteuil's little phrase" which is associated by
Swann with his love for Odette. Swann comes to know Odette and
the musical phrase at about the same time, and identifies them with
each other. The first reference is made by M. Verdurin, to "the
sonata in F sharp which we have discovered," which Mme Verdurin
calls "her sonata."[14] This is followed by the pianist's playing of the
sonata, and then a lengthy evocation of Swann's earlier encounter
with it and the pleasure he derived from "the mass of the piano
part, multiform, coherent, level, and breaking everywhere in
melody like the mauve agitation of the sea, silvered and charmed
into a minor key by the moonlight":[15] "He was like a man into
whose life a woman, whom he has seen for a moment passing by,
has brought a new form of beauty."[16] This musical phrase he had
fallen in love with, with its "mauve agitation," is soon associated
with Odette, whose favorite color is mauve, as we have seen; it
becomes "the national hymn of their love." It is played either by
violin and piano or at the piano alone, either by the pianist at the
Verdurins' or, on occasion, by Odette herself. Swann clings to it for
consolation when he sees her attracted by Forcheville; later, when
she avoids him, the chance hearing of the phrase first causes him
great pain, and then seems to console him by speaking to him of
Odette. The phrase is personified, compassionate, full of wisdom.
Much later, in *The Sweet Cheat Gone (La Fugitive)*, the narrator
will refer to the same musical phrase, which Albertine had often
played for him on the piano, and which he identifies with his lost
love for her.

The narrator speaks of "many other sensations I have mentioned, which had seemed to me to be synthesized in the last works of Vinteuil."[17] This special role assigned to music finds clear expression in the following passage:

And thinking over again that timeless joy caused by the sound of the spoon or the taste of the *madeleine*, I said to myself, "Was that the happiness suggested by the little phrase of the sonata to Swann, who made the mistake of confusing it with the pleasure of love and was unable to find it in artistic creation—that happiness which I came to sense dimly was even farther removed from everything earthly than the little phrase of the sonata had suggested, when I caught the red, mysterious call of that septet which Swann had never known, having died, like so many others, before the truth intended for them had been revealed?" But it would have availed him nothing in any case, for that phrase may, indeed, have been able to symbolize a call, but it could not have created talents and made of Swann the writer he never was.[18]

It is indeed mostly in connection with the composer Vinteuil and his works that music appears in the novel. In the volume following the episode of Swann's love-affair with Odette, there is a long and significant passage on the interrelationship between music, memory, and the work of Vinteuil.[19]

Another link between love and music is established by the use of metaphorical spatialization. Swann is amazed at the power of words, "mere words, words uttered in the air, at a distance." The spatialization of love is effected especially in *The Sweet Cheat Gone (La Fugitive)*. The chief passages concerning the spatialization of music are to be found, on the contrary, in *Swann's Way (Du côté de chez Swann)*, in the episode entitled *Swann in Love (Un amour de Swann)*: "Presumably the notes which we hear at such moments tend to spread out before our eyes, over surfaces greater or smaller according to their pitch and volume; to trace arabesque designs, to give us the sensation of breadth or tenuity, stability or caprice. . . . He was able to picture to himself its extent, its symmetrical arrangement, its notation, the strength of its expression; he had before him that definite object which was no longer pure music, but rather design, architecture, thought, and which allowed the actual music to be recalled."[20]

IV *Art and Alienation*

Whereas music, especially classical music, involves repetition and therefore requires the play of memory, the plastic arts have a more immediate impact, stemming partly from the primacy and immediacy of sight compared with our other senses, partly from the fact that the eye can embrace a painting as a whole in one glance—a feat the ear cannot accomplish for a piece of music. However, just as the ear can, *after* hearing a piece through, elaborate from the successive details a synthetic or totalizing grasp of it as a whole, so the eye, after the first general glance at the picture, will (reversing the process) proceed to run from detail to detail in a successive manner. In other words, whereas in the perception of music the syntagmatic dimension precedes the systematic, in the perception of painting that sequence is reversed.

Whereas music, being repetitious, is used by the narrator as a symbol of memory, painting, being artificially (that is, two-dimensionally) representational, is used as a symbol of alienation. Thus Swann's alienation from the immediate reality of people is indicated by his seeing them in terms of picture characters, which both reduces them to conformity to static, two-dimensional stereotypes and relegates them to the past—the past of the painter's depiction of the model, the past of Swann's first acquaintance with the painted figure of which the real person is merely a reminiscence. The real interests him not insofar as it is particular and unique but insofar as it conforms to an aesthetic ideal.

We are told a number of times about Swann's "moral aridity," and it would appear to be connected with his lack of creativity. He takes refuge from ideals and elevated ideas in the pursuit of everyday satisfactions, preferring the material and the superficial. Swann is a man "whose eyes, although delicate interpreters of painting, whose mind, although an acute observer of manners, must bear for ever the indelible imprint of the barrenness of his life."[21] Under the influence of his milieu (the skeptical coterie of the Princesse des Laumes) and of his age, Swann becomes one of those men "who, instead of externalizing the objects of their aspirations, endeavour to separate from the accumulation of the years already spent a definite residue of habits and passions which they can regard as characteristic and permanent"[22]—"a positive, almost a medical philosophy."[23] At one time, Odette absent, he does not think of her, "as though this moral distance were proportionate to the physical distance"[24]—but this is a reversal of the usual pattern, in which presence calms (indeed, weakens) the attraction, while absence exasperates it.

The narrator sees in a carriage "a funeral car on some Pompeïan terra-cotta," and in the horizon "the back-ground of a Japanese print."[25] He declares that the so-called "realist" literature is in fact *unrealistic* because a merely factual description of things eliminates the memory-based aura which they have for us. The passage of Time can only be represented by "a sort of psychology of space."[26]

Swann's alienation is shared by the narrator. The narrator sees Andrée as the *Idolatry* of Giotto, while Swann sees in the scullery-maid the same painter's *Charity*.[27] Whereas the narrator sees in Odette a Watteau, Swann, his alter ego, sees in her the daughter of Jethro in the fresco of the *Life of Moses*, or a Botticelli: "He still liked to recognize in his wife one of Botticelli's figures. Odette, who on the contrary sought not to bring out but to make up for, to cover and conceal, the points in herself that did not please her, what might perhaps to an artist express her 'character,' but in her woman's eyes were merely blemishes, would not have that painter mentioned in her presence. Swann had a wonderful scarf of oriental silk, blue and pink, which he had bought because it was exactly that worn by Our Lady in the *Magnificat*. But Mme Swann refused to wear it."[28] This resistance on the part of Odette to her assimilation to a painted figure may well reflect in part a fear of objectification, of reification by Swann, which depersonalizes the object of the gaze.

There appears to be a very deliberate attempt on the part of the narrator, as writer, to compete with his painter Elstir in depicting the objects of everyday life and transforming them by the alchemy of his creative artistry:

Since I had seen such things depicted in water-colours by Elstir, I sought to find again in reality, I cherished, as though for their poetic beauty, the broken gestures of the knives still lying across one another, the swollen convexity of a discarded napkin upon which the sun would patch a scrap of yellow velvet, the half-empty glass which thus showed to greater advantage the noble sweep of its curved sides, and, in the heart of its translucent crystal, clear as frozen daylight, a dreg of wine, dusky but sparkling with reflected lights, the displacement of solid objects, the transmutation of liquids by the effect of light and shade, the shifting colour of the plums which passed from green to blue and from blue to golden yellow in the half-plundered dish, the chairs, like a group of old ladies, that came twice daily to take their places round the white cloth spread on the table as on an altar at which were celebrated the rites of the palate, where in the hollows of oyster-shells a few drops of lustral water had gathered as in tiny holy water stoups of stone; I tried to find beauty there where I had never imagined before that it could exist, in the most ordinary things, in the profundities of "still life."[29]

Another subject of such transmutation is the picnic he shares with the group of girls: "My friends preferred the sandwiches, and were surprised to see me eat only a single chocolate cake, sugared with gothic tracery, or an apricot tart. This was because, with the sandwiches of cheese or of greenstuff, a form of food that was novel to me and knew nothing of the past, I had nothing in common. But the cakes understood, the tarts were gossips. There were in the former an insipid taste of cream, in the latter a fresh taste of fruit which knew all about Combray, and about Gilberte, not only the Gilberte of Combray but her too of Paris, at whose tea-parties I had found them again."[30]

It is striking that in such passages the artistic transformation takes essentially the form of anthropomorphosis and desecularization. Perhaps the latter tendency explains the large role given, in the *Recherche*, to religious art: the stained-glass windows and the tapestries of Saint-Hilaire, the sculptures of Saint-André-des-Champs, the porch of the church of Balbec, the paintings of Giotto or El Greco or Gustave Moreau.

The most important reflections on painting, however, are made in connection with the character Elstir, which we shall deal with in the next chapter.

While many objects have a traditional archetypal significance, and others are specifically endowed with a more transitory symbolic function, yet others in the *Recherche* play an important role without moving beyond their everyday sphere. This role, based on repetition, is that of catalyst, played by the tea-soaked *madeleine*, an uneven paving-stone, a starched napkin, the sound of a water pipe or of a spoon striking against a plate. Here a later sensation recalls a former and with it evokes an instant of being (and sensing) outside of time—much as metaphor brings two elements together artistically in such a way as to transcend space and categorization. In his conquest of time, the protagonist is inhibited by his father but aided and abetted by Albertine. He discovers that habit, like love with its gift of knowledge paid for with suffering, is a two-edged sword, dulling pain and fear and the passage of time only at the price of insensitivity and unconsciousness. The pain of remembering, like the pain of jealousy, must be accepted and borne. Both are intimately associated with music, notably that of Vinteuil, and especially through the episode of Swann's affair with Odette. Swann, in his reaction to music as in his seeing people as artworks, is a model of the protagonist, but a failed model because not creative: the protagonist transcends his alienation by becoming his own narrator and writing a masterpiece: the *Recherche*.

CHAPTER 9

Art

I *The World and the Word*

LANGUAGE, written and spoken, constitutes not only the texture of the *Recherche* but a fundamental theme. Thus, except for a passing allusion to the bedside lamp, the first mention of external reality is of the filtered, artificial reality of literature, and the alienating effect of such reading is stressed: "I would try to put away the book which, I imagined, was still in my hands, and to blow out the light; I had been thinking all the time, while I was asleep, of what I had just been reading, but my thoughts had run into a channel of their own, until I myself seemed actually to have become the subject of my book: a church, a quartet, the rivalry between François I and Charles V."[1] Other written texts are soon mentioned—the writings of Saint-Simon, the *Pensées* of Pascal—and the question of the influence of the texts one reads returns with greater emphasis: for the narrator's name day, his grandmother "had at first chosen Musset's poems, a volume of Rousseau, and *Indiana;* for while she considered light reading as unwholesome as sweets and cakes, she did not reflect that the strong breath of genius must have upon the very soul of a child an influence at once more dangerous and less quickening than those of fresh air and country breezes upon his body. But when my father had seemed almost to regard her as insane on learning the names of the books she proposed to give me, she had journeyed back by herself to Jouy-le-Vicomte to the bookseller's, and had decided upon the four pastoral novels of George Sand."[2] The *Recherche* contains many references to literary figures—Racine, Mme de Sévigné, Mme de Lafayette, the Goncourts, and so on—and comments on the significance of style in literature: "Style is for the writer, as for the painter, a question not of technique but of vision."[3]

Literary examples are not the only ones given for written language: newspapers are mentioned—*Les Débats roses, Le Figaro*—as are letters from Gisèle, to and from Albertine, from Aimé. He dwells with pleasure on the tender tone he finds in letters from girl-friends, but complains nevertheless at how little of a person is present in his or her letters.

Writing can take on a very active function, in fact represent an action: his letter to his mother is so important to him that years later when recording the incident he compares her reply "There is no answer" to that sent to an unwanted woman by the man to whom she has written; and it is by letter that Swann declares to the narrator's father that he no longer loves Odette.

The effect of reading a written text is evoked on a number of occasions. He writes upon reading some pages of the Goncourts' *Journal:* "I might, perhaps, have concluded from them that life teaches us to set a lower value on reading . . . but I might quite as well have concluded that, on the contrary, reading teaches us to set a higher value on life."[4] Reading is presented as creative, for the reader's participation in the text as process is far from passive: "Each reader reads only what is already within himself. The book is only a sort of optical instrument which the writer offers to the reader to enable the latter to discover in himself what he would not have found but for the aid of the book."[5] A doubly significant example of this is provided very early in the work: with what emotion does the narrator recall the exquisite sensibility and sureness of taste with which his mother read to him the works of George Sand! And he remarks of the great actors of the time that their art, "although as yet I had no experience of it, was the first of all its numberless forms in which Art itself allowed me to anticipate its enjoyment."[6] This art is, of course, an art of transformation: his mother "smoothed away, as she read on, any harshness there might be or discordance in the tenses of verbs, . . . and breathed into this quite ordinary prose a kind of life, continuous and full of feeling."[7]

Reading is discussed several other times, as in Gisèle's letter relating her examination exercise (a letter from Sophocles to Racine) and discussed by Albertine and Andrée or the telegram first believed to be from Albertine (previously thought to be dead) and later realized to have been from Gilberte. He comments: "We guess as we read, we create."

The distinction between written and spoken language (*écriture* and *parole*) is evoked not only functionally but also stylistically: he notes that Mme de Cambremer uses expressions "which would have been more appropriate to the written language, a distinction that she did not perceive, for she derived them more from reading than from conversation." Words can substitute for sight, in a form of oral literature—neither primitive, however, nor even innocent—which constitutes not communication, as in most other types of oral expression, but invention: "She was charming when she invented a story which left no room for doubt, for one saw then in front of oneself the thing—albeit imaginary—which she was saying, using it as an illustration of her speech."[8]

The limitations of spoken language lead to amusing or frustrating misunderstandings—as in the case of the grandmother's sisters: "They, in their horror of vulgarity, had brought to such a fine art the concealment of a personal allusion in a wealth of ingenious circumlocution, that it would often pass unnoticed even by the person to whom it was addressed." They, on the other hand, cannot imagine that their compliments are not as obvious to the person to whom they are addressed as to themselves—an error similar to that made by the narrator which causes the break with his Uncle Adolphe.[9]

A further curious characteristic of spoken language is what is seen by the speaker as the danger of appearing pedantic—a fear that unites the cultivated Swann to the uncultured Françoise. Thus Swann, having mentioned Pascal's *Pensées*, "articulated the title with an ironic emphasis so as not to appear pedantic"; similarly Françoise, having had occasion to mention X-rays, "pronounced 'x' with an affectation of difficulty and with a smile in deprecation of her, an unlettered woman's daring to employ a scientific term."[10]

The use of a foreign language (English) between Odette and Gilberte inspires this reflection: "In a language that we know, we have substituted for the opacity of sounds the perspicuity of ideas."[11] This, of course, is merely another observation on the multiple effects of habit, so often mentioned for its tendency to distract our attention from the sensual texture of reality.

II   Nature versus Culture

The *Recherche* is rich in the evocation of natural objects and scenes: flowers, hedges, trees in bloom, landscapes, seascapes. However, while the narrator is clearly very sensitive to these stimuli, it is striking that he relates to them primarily through transformation, which is essentially metaphorical.

The most obvious type of metaphor used recalls the definition of culture given by Claude Lévi-Strauss: culture is man added to nature. These metaphors, in other words, are examples of anthropomorphosis, man being precisely "added to" nature by the narrator's imaginative transformation.

A second type (or level) of metaphor associates nature with the profane, culture with the sacred—as in the flowers (natural, profane) and their imaginative transformation into figures especially garbed for the celebration of religious ritual (cultural, sacred).

But the distinction between nature and culture is reflected here primarily in the relationship between nature and art. Thus the theme of eclosion (often associated with the symbol of the lotus) is presented first through the description of the Japanese water-papers and then very shortly afterward through the example of the dried lime tea leaves—the natural vehicle of the theme being thus preceded by its artistic vehicle. Here the distinction between the natural and the artificial (because artistic) is submerged—and elsewhere it is expressly denied, as in the assimilation of "works of genius" to "nature itself when the hand of man had not . . . trimmed it." There appears to be a weakness for the natural in the assertion that great art is transparent. Particularly characteristic is the tendency to reduce natural phenomena, such as flowers, to artistic ones, and analogous is the reduction of real people (the Guermantes) to artificial artworks.[12]

The divorce between art and life does appear, however—as in the contrasting views of real-life family ties, which are de-emphasized, and their portrayal in literature. Again, in the reference to "[the] lack of harmony between our impressions and their normal forms of expression," the narrator adverts to the mediating and alienating character of both the language available to us (*langue*) and our use of it (*parole*).

The cultural transformation of nature (or the artistic transformation of the real) may be seen in the transcendence of everyday reality by means of the metamorphosis of imagery. Thus his Aunt Léonie is assimilated to Louis XIV (through her manic attention to the insignificant details of her daily routine), suppressing the centuries as well as the social barriers which separate her from the Sun King. The books of the author Bergotte, who trades his life for the sight of a little piece of painted yellow wall in a painting by Ver Meer, keep watch by his bier and symbolize his resurrection. The role of images is emphasized by the narrator: "An image presented by life brings us in reality at that moment multiple and varying sen-

sations. . . . An hour is not merely an hour, it is a vase filled with
perfumes, sounds, plans, and climates. . . . Truth will begin only
when the writer takes two different objects, establishes their
relationship—analogous in the world of art to the sole relationship
in the world of science, the law of cause and effect—and encloses
them in the necessary rings of a beautiful style, . . . in a
metaphor."[13]

This transformation is seen as a great boon by the grandmother:
"She attempted by a subterfuge, if not to eliminate altogether their
commercial banality, at least to minimize it, to substitute for the
bulk of it what was art still, to introduce, as it might be, several
'thicknesses' of art; instead of photographs of Chartres Cathedral, of
the Fountain of Saint-Cloud, or of Vesuvius, she would enquire of
Swann whether some great painter had not made pictures of them,
and preferred to give me photographs of 'Chartres Cathedral' after
Corot, of the 'Fountains of Saint-Cloud' after Hubert Robert, and
of 'Vesuvius' after Turner, which were a stage higher in the scale of
art."[14]

A certain art of transformation is also attributed by the narrator to
the actress and the *cocotte*: "They devote all their generosity, all
their talent, their transferable dreams of sentimental beauty . . .
and their gold, which counts for little, to the fashioning of a fine
and precious setting for the rubbed and scratched and ill-polished
lives of men." Such a perspective is surprising and a little disturbing—and so are other views of artistic metamorphosis. It can, for example, be at times quite alienating: "I cannot express the discom-
fort I felt at such an intrusion of mystery and beauty into a room
which I had succeeded in filling with my own personality. . . . The doorhandle of my room, which was different to me
from all other doorhandles in the world, inasmuch as it seemed to
open of its own accord and without my having to turn it, . . . lo
and behold, it was now an astral body for Golo." The disturbing
character of the transformations of art are even more clearly indicated in the following passage: "A 'sadist' of her kind is an artist
in evil, which a wholly wicked person could not be, for in that case
the evil would not have been external, it would have seemed quite
natural to her."[15]

Legrandin tells the young protagonist that he has "a pretty soul,
of rare quality, an artist's nature"; Bergotte remarks: "You are ill,
but you are not to be pitied, because you have intellectual satisfactions."[16] And indeed much artistry is displayed in the narrator's
evocation of the midday meal at Aunt Léonie's prepared by

Françoise and of the asparagus seen in the kitchen[17]—to limit ourselves here to the very early years. But the passages on the artistic talent of prostitutes and sadists throw a somewhat dubious light on the narrator's "artistic nature."

III *Literature as Vocation, Literature as Art*

There are many reflections on the art of writing. "The ingenuity of the first novelist lay in his understanding that, as the picture was the one essential element in the complicated structure of our emotions, so that simplification of it which consisted in the suppression, pure and simple, of 'real' people would be a decided improvement."[18] Swann declares that " 'Life' contains situations more interesting and more romantic than all the romances ever written."[19] The narrator jokes about the businessman's disdainful attitude of superiority toward those who spend their time reading or writing, even if the result is a masterpiece like *Hamlet*. He characterizes nineteenth-century writers (Balzac, Hugo, Michelet) as essentially incomplete, but as deriving unity and grandeur from the author's view of his own work, which leads, for example, a Balzac to unite his novels in the single cycle of the *Human Comedy*.

The protagonist declares (to Charlus): "I adore certain symbols as much as you. But it would be absurd for the sake of the symbol to sacrifice the reality it represents."[20] On the other hand, he remarks several times the dislocation between our impressions and our manner of expressing them, and as a writer he declares himself for "idealism," which he defines as the realization (based on experience) of the unimportance of material reality, into which anything can be placed by the operations of the mind. This transmutation is exemplified by rich imagery: "My love, which had just seen and recognized the one enemy by whom it could be conquered, forgetfulness, began to tremble, like a lion which in the cage in which it has been confined has suddenly caught sight of the python that will devour it."[21] Psychological complexity is reflected in long sentences with series of additions and modifications, in the joining of a number of parallel expressions.

In spite of all this conscious artistry, he declares that "we are not at all free in the presence of the work of art to be created," that "we do not do it as we ourselves please."[22] Nor can we appreciate great art and literature until we have achieved a certain level of maturity.[23]

Ordinary language can describe banal, everyday things ("this sort of residue of experience"), but significant experience, which is more intimate and hard to express, requires (and thus justifies) the stylistic effort of a great writer, which is in fact an effort of "translation." His literary vocation preoccupies the narrator from an early age. He worries about "this want of talent, this black cavity which gaped in my mind when I ransacked it for the theme of my future writings," which augurs ill for his ambition to be "the first writer of my day": "It was evident to me then that . . . I was to be distinguished merely as one of those who have no aptitude for writing. And so, utterly despondent, I renounced literature for ever."[24] He attributes his inability to settle down to writing first to his frustration at not being able to see Gilberte, then to the distraction caused by visiting her. In any case, sure that he will begin tomorrow, he does not feel obliged to worry about not beginning today—and of course tomorrow never comes. Later in life he blames it on ingrained habits which dominate his ways of life. He muses on the literary vocation of a Mme de Villeparisis; his reading of the Goncourts' *Journal* almost reconciles him with not writing, because it suggests that literature reveals no deeper truth, but he rejects this notion when he recognizes the inspiration he derives from the perception of what two beings have in common with each other.[25] This idea does come back to haunt him still later, however: "I could no longer hope to find joy in literature, whether through my own fault, for lack of talent, or because literature itself was less pregnant with reality then I had thought."[26] The narrator's vocation is of course confirmed for us by innumerable passages, of which perhaps the most striking from a purely stylistic point of view are the landscapes and seascapes he paints, or a fine still life.

The mode of perception may be similar in both writing and painting; he says of Mme. de Sévigné: "I realised at Balbec that it was in the same way as he [the painter Elstir, 'who had such a profound influence on my way of seeing things'] that she presented things to her readers, in the order of our perception of them, instead of first having to explain them in relation to their several causes."[27] When he visits fashionable *salons* like that of Mme. de Montmorency, his aim is not "to take notes" or "to make a study."[28]

He laments the confusion of high moral themes with true literary value in a work, whereas purely formal beauty demands a much deeper turning inward upon oneself. The true subject is the reality which the details of our existence separate us from, namely, our life; and "real life is literature." He has a revelation: "I understood that all these materials for literary work were nothing else than my past life. . . . And so my entire life up to that day could—and, from another point of view, could not—be summed up under the title: *A Vocation.*"[29]

Much of the treatment of literature is centered on the figure of the writer Bergotte. This character is first mentioned as being recommended to the protagonist by Bloch, who derides his comrade's taste for Musset's *Nuit d'octobre* and prefers Bergotte because he is recommended by Leconte de Lisle. Soon the protagonist develops a personal taste for Bergotte, based on his particular philosophy and style—unusual phrases, bursts of music, idealist philosophy. He finds in Bergotte's works the tone of "a frail and disappointed old man, who had lost his children and had never found any consolation."[30] M. de Norpois has a different way of putting it: for him, Bergotte is "a fine intellect who [plunges] us into otiose and byzantine discussions of the merits of pure form": "It is all very precious, very thin, and has very little virility," "all these Chinese puzzles of form, all these delinquescent mandarin subtleties." According to Norpois, "one finds [in his books] nothing but perpetual and, between ourselves, somewhat wearisome analyses, torturing scruples, morbid remorse, and all for the merest peccadilloes, the most trivial naughtinesses."[31] The protagonist's views remain unchanged: he finds in Bergotte "a sweet and divine wisdom" and an insistence on "the endless torrent of appearances." His style is marked by "closing phrases where the accumulated sounds are prolonged," and his last novels were "full of a regard for what was right and proper so painfully rigid that the most innocent pleasures of their heroes were poisoned by it."[32] Bergotte justifies the large sums of money he gives to young girls on the basis of the literary inspiration they then provide him with; failing in health, he eventually ceases to leave his apartment. One feels more and more, especially toward the end, how many traits are shared by Bergotte and the narrator.

IV *The Magic Lanterns of Art, Music, and Literature*

The *Recherche* contains much speculation on art: "That ineffable something which makes a difference in quality between what each of us has felt . . . , art, the art of a Vinteuil like that of an Elstir, expresses it."[33] He treasures "the promise that there existed something other, realisable no doubt by art, than the nullity that I had found in all my pleasures and in love itself."[34] He likes to mix various sense impressions, mingling with the music of Vinteuil the beauty of Albertine, comparing Dostoevski with Rembrandt and with an ancient frieze. He complains of being forced, by the "deceptive brevity of this volume," to deform the infinitely extensive reality he portrays. One art can drive out another: his passion for tragedy is shifted to Gothic tapestries and modern paintings.

He speaks of "that sort of tenderness, of solemn sweetness in the pomp of a joyful celebration, which characterize certain pages of *Lohengrin*, certain paintings by Carpaccio, and makes us understand how Baudelaire was able to apply to the sound of the trumpet the epithet 'delicious.' "[35] His own fictitious artists form a similar trio of representatives of the sister arts: "I would take up an album of Elstir's work, one of Bergotte's books, Vinteuil's sonata."[36] In these trios, we find a taste for synaesthesia which surfaces elsewhere also: "What I like about these foodstuffs that are cried is that a thing which we hear like a rhapsody changes its nature when it comes to our table and addresses itself to my palate. As for ices . . . , it is like an illustrated geography book which I look at first of all and then convert its raspberry or vanilla monuments into coolness in my throat."[37] We have already evoked Bergotte: Elstir and Vinteuil also are important elements.

In the plastic arts, he mentions Gustave Moreau, Hubert Robert, and the fictitious Elstir. Elstir is the only person known to Robert whose intelligence is comparable to that of the protagonist. "He had started with mythological subjects . . . , and had then been for long under the influence of Japanese art," before beginning to paint "landscapes and still life," "a real thaw, an authentic square in a country town, live women on a beach." The narrator says of Elstir's paintings:

Among these pictures several of the kind that seemed most absurd to ordinary people interested me more than the rest because they recreated those optical illusions which prove to us that we should never succeed in identifying objects if we did not make some process of reasoning intervene. How often, when driving in the dark, do we not come upon a long, lighted street which begins a few feet away from us, when what we have actually before our eyes is nothing but a rectangular patch of wall with a bright light falling on it, which has given us the mirage of depth. In view of which is it not logical, not by any artifice of symbolism but by a sincere return to the very root of the impression, to represent one thing by that other for which, in the flash of a first illusion, we mistook it? Surfaces and volumes are in reality independent of the names of objects which our memory imposes on them after we have recognized them. Elstir attempted to wrest from what he had just felt what he already knew, his effort had often been to break up that aggregate of impressions which we call vision.[38]

One of the great attractions of Elstir's work for the protagonist is a trait in common with Bergotte—the "torrent of appearances": the painter "had had the skill to arrest for all time the motion of the hours at this luminous instant, when the lady had felt hot and had stopped dancing, when the tree was fringed with a belt of shadow, when the sails seemed to be slipping over a golden glaze. But just because the depicted moment pressed on one with so much force, this so permanent canvas gave one the most fleeting impression, one felt that the lady would presently move out of it, the boats drift away, the night draw on, that pleasure comes to an end, that life passes and that the moments illuminated by the convergence, at once, of so many lights do not recur."[39] Elstir could not observe (or paint) a flower "without first transplanting it to that inner garden in which we are obliged always to remain":[40] so much for mimesis.

Music is evoked a number of times, and precisely the same image is used as for Elstir: that of the magic lantern.[41] Central importance is given to the work of the fictitious composer Vinteuil. I have dealt elsewhere with the "little phrase" associated by Swann with his love for Odette; the protagonist further associates Vinteuil's sonata with various emotions. He is struck, as with Elstir, by Vinteuil's unique vision as transmitted in his works. He also describes the evolution of his appreciation for the work of Vinteuil, whose use of the motif of the bells at first displeases him but later becomes the element he prefers. Vinteuil's concert piece suggests to him the possibility of achieving his goal of recovering lost time, and the mysterious pleasure—"coming not from a memory but from an impression"[42]—associated with the *madeleine*, the trees, and the bell-towers appears to be synthesized in the composer's last works.[43]

There is a dilution of the "magic lantern" comparison from painting, where it is "the head of the artist [Elstir],"[44] to music, where it is "the pianola":[45] the passage from image to image symbolizes first the movement from one Elstir painting to another, then that from composer to composer. The application to literature is even more diluted: memory is like a magic lantern and the many different images the lantern shows resemble the many different Albertines he recalls and which he will describe in the *Recherche*.[46]

With reference to the content and method of literature, the narrator opposes ideas to gossip, essence to existence, theory to

phenomena: however, he rejects both phenomena, because transient, and theory, because abstract, preferring art. He prefers connotation to denotation, intuition to discursive reasoning. Essences
cannot be deduced, must be intuited, and nothing is more precious
than an intuition of this sort. In certain remarks about money,
women, and the literary vocation, he shows a tendency to make the
most fragile generalizations about life and literature on the basis of
his own very particular experience[47]—and later specifically attempts
to discount this particularity by adducing other examples than
himself, such as Chateaubriand, Nerval, Baudelaire. Thus the
weakness for abusive generalizations which we encountered in his
discussion of love reappears in his treatment of the arts, especially
literature.

If the *Recherche* is about memory and oblivion, time and eter-
nity, life and death, it is also about reality and art. Each of the arts
is treated, with much attention devoted to both painting and music,
but the narrator's chief concern is with the art of literature and the
literary vocation. In fact, if time is to be recaptured, oblivion and
death defeated, it will be through art, and especially that of
literature. Nature is life, and life leads to death; only through
culture, through art, can mortality be opposed. True art is a matter
not of great moral themes, which are relative and ephemeral, but of
a formal perfection in which a deep wisdom is clothed in the
evanescent, iridescent beauty of the phenomenal world. The artist's
vision, or series of visions, is symbolized by the magic lantern.

CHAPTER 10

Roots

I *Other Works and Literary Affiliations*

PROUST began as a dilettante, contributing portraits, sketches, and criticism to the review *Le Banquet* founded in 1892 by the frequenters of Mme Strauss' salon, where Proust was often seen in the last lustrum of the nineteenth century. He collected these pieces and a few others in a volume entitled *Les Plaisirs et les jours* which he published in 1896 a few months after his plaquette *Portraits de peintres.*

Les Plaisirs et les jours, in spite of a style which was too flowery and cloying, larded to excess with abstractions and symbols, nevertheless revealed certain qualities of grace and facility which suggested the possibility of a future talent of real promise. The artist and his models are still intimately related by a common experience (reflected, precisely, in the language employed), but the future satires of the *Recherche* are already present in embryonic form.

The years 1896 to 1904 were devoted to a novel, *Jean Santeuil,* which was long to remain unpublished but is important because it constitutes the first sketch of the *Recherche.* Apparently not yet fully master of his materials and his message, Proust attempts to justify lack of cohesion and finish by means of the traditional convention of the unfinished manuscript. Another weakness by comparison with the *Recherche* is the lack of the remarkable progress in understanding and wisdom (concerning, for example, the status of our relationship with external, inanimate "reality") evident in the mature work. But certain traits of the latter are already detectable in the narcissism of the protagonist, his pride and sensitivity, his fear of humiliation, the anguish of jealousy, his precarious health, his predilection for enclosed spaces.

There followed translations of John Ruskin with Proust's elaborate and significant prefaces and notes (1904 and 1906). The

127

years from 1908 to 1910 saw a series of pastiches (of Honoré de Balzac, Gustave Flaubert, Henri de Régnier, the Goncourt brothers, Jules Michelet, Emile Faguet, Ernest Renan, Henri de Saint-Simon), published in the *Figaro* from February, 1908, to March, 1909, and collected in 1919 in a volume entitled *Pastiches et mélanges.* The "mélanges," which constitute three-quarters of the volume, consist of a long essay on French cathedrals (inspired by Ruskin), a short piece (a dozen pages) entitled "Sentiments familiaux d'un parricide," and a final section given the heading "Journées de lecture."

In 1909 he begins his *Contre Sainte-Beuve,* a critical essay in the form of a novel. The preface contains (in fact, consists of) a declaration of the inferiority of *l'intelligence* compared to *l'instinct* and *les secrets du sentiment,* a declaration which situates Proust in the tradition of Pierre de Marivaux and Blaise Pascal. He develops this idea by means of elements which will reappear in the *Recherche:* magical resurrections provoked by the taste of a piece of toast soaked in tea, the sensation of stepping on uneven paving-stones, the sound of a spoon striking a plate, the sight of a group of trees. The actual text of *Contre Sainte-Beuve* will also contain many elements, such as the article in the *Figaro,* which will reappear in the mature work. But the central idea is the following: "Sainte-Beuve's work is lacking in depth. The famous method . . . , which consists in not separating the man and the work, . . . ignores what any attentive observation of ourselves teaches us: that a book is the product of another self from that which we reveal in our habits, in society, in our vices." What Charles-Augustin Sainte-Beuve has failed to realize is that "the writer's self reveals itself only in his books."[1] In rejecting Sainte-Beuve, Proust inaugurated the literary criticism of our day as it came to be developed by Anglo-American New Criticism, culminating in a work like *The Verbal Ikon* with its emphasis on the principle of immanence.

Much has been written of the various influences experienced by Proust.[2] That of Saint-Simon is of course explicit and fundamental: both studied the society of a period just past in a vast fresco, with a wealth of detailed observation and of striking portraits, stressing the fact that the truth is hidden behind misleading appearances that must be penetrated by the psychologist and moralist. The relationship with Rousseau is more complex, for the *Confessions* are not a novel as the *Recherche* is: however, the division of the *moi* is remarkable in both—the narrator and the protagonist recall

Rousseau *judge of* Jean-Jacques—as is the refuge in solitude and
the imagination, the emphasis on involuntary memory (Rousseau's
pervenche) and on the theme of time. Proust's place in the tradition
of the psychological novel relates him to Mme de La Fayette before
linking him with Stendhal.

A more interesting and elusive connection, perhaps, is that which
relates Proust to Marivaux and Michel de Montaigne. In many
ways, this is simply a further illustration of the affiliation that runs
from mannerism (Montaigne) through the rococo (Marivaux) to impressionism (Proust), an affiliation so well established in the plastic
arts. In each, we have a long, meandering sentence used for subtle
psychological exploration and lucid evocation of the passions which
is virtually eclipsed in the seventeenth and nineteenth centuries.
Again the division of the self, the love of society (even snobbery).

Although his mature writing was done in the twentieth century,
Proust has many links with the nineteenth century in which he was
born. Like the great romantics, he sees the imagination as truly
creative, and indeed many general conceptions and tendencies
relate him to them; but there are also other, more specific ties.
Some of them are expressly indicated by the narrator: "Was it not
from sensations of the same sort as I received from the *madeleine*
that the most beautiful part of the *Mémoires d'Outre-Tombe* was
derived? . . . One of the masterpieces of French literature, the
Sylvie of Gérard de Nerval, like the *Mémoires d'Outre-Tombe*
which tell of Combourg, contains a sensation of the same character
as the savour of the *madeleine* or the 'trilling of the lark.' And finally, in Baudelaire, these reminiscences are still more frequent and
obviously less incidental and therefore, in my opinion, decisive."[3]

His contribution to the psychology of love builds on Stendhal's
theory of crystallization or accretion as developed in *De l'amour*.
Balzac, another Titan dead at the age of fifty-one, provided him
with the example of a great social historian who was also more a
visionary than a mere observer. Like Emile Zola, another great
novelist of the nineteenth century, he began his great work just
before the destruction of the society he was to portray, so that he
found himself, by an accident of fate, describing social realities
which no longer belonged to the present but to the historical past.

Finally we must mention the example of two foreign writers:
Henry James, the subtle, artistic, psychological portraitist of the upper classes, with his passionate interest in the theory of the novel,
and John Ruskin, the idealistic initiator into the profound beauty

and meaning of Gothic France and "Oriental" Venice. Both, but
particularly Ruskin, exerted a considerable influence on Proust, as
evidenced by many pages of the *Recherche*.

II *A Generation of Giants*

Rarely has a single country produced within the brief span of four
years so brilliant and diverse a group of writers as was born in
France between 1868 and 1871: the poet and dramatist Paul
Claudel, the novelist André Gide, the poet-theorist Paul Valéry, and
the novelist-critic Marcel Proust. The paths of these four were
destined to cross, almost inevitably—sometimes spectacularly, as in
the attempts of the militant Catholic Claudel to proselytize Gide, or
in the latter's monumental error of judgment in rejecting for
publication the manuscript of Proust's masterpiece *Remembrance
of Things Past (A la recherche du temps perdu)*. However, none of
the four owed his fame to the fact that his birth happened to coïn-
cide with that of the other three: to a much greater degree than the
most celebrated classical and romantic writers, each of these four
moderns is a great writer not as part of a group but in his own right,
and of none is this more true than of Marcel Proust.

Born at the very moment when Claude Monet and Pierre-
Auguste Renoir, in the aftermath of the Franco-Prussian War, were
inventing impressionist painting, which marked the beginning of
the modern period in art, Proust—followed by James Joyce (b.
1882), Franz Kafka (b. 1883), and William Faulkner (b. 1897)—was
to usher in the modern period in the novel.

Proust's generation inherited a language which had recently experienced a radical review at the hands of poets like Stéphane
Mallarmé and Lautréamont. This reworking had a drastic effect
which made the language of a Zola inadequate and irrelevant to
modern needs; and while its effects are no doubt most obvious in
the poetry of Valéry and Claudel and in the theater of the latter,
they, together with the influence of Joris-Karl Huysmans and Oscar
Wilde, are detectable also in the fiction of Gide and especially
Proust, at once the most subtle and the most sumptuous French
prose writer of the early twentieth century.

The Dreyfus case, which must of course be seen in the light of the
humiliating and rankling defeat suffered by France at the hands of
Bismarck in the Franco-Prussian War, caused a vast crisis whose
ramifications went far beyond the political sphere, into the racial,

the religious, the financial. They also, by straining and breaking old ties and fostering new ones, and by redrawing alliances generally, disturbed many sacrosanct customs, taboos, and shibboleths of a purely social character. It is this that is so brilliantly portrayed in the middle volumes of the *Recherche,* and it is the Dreyfus case that situates the work most clearly on the historical level and in the history of French social evolution. The "case" will find other chroniclers, such as Martin du Gard whose *Jean Barois* centers on the role played by Emile Zola, but none will explore more brilliantly, more subtly, or more discreetly the endless complexity of the less obvious social effects of the whole affair and the forces of polarization it set in motion. The confusion caused by the case and the subsequent financial chaos caused by World War I bring to an end a whole society of which Proust is the unequaled analyst and portraitist. Proust alone, of the four giants of his generation, has given us a rich and profound analysis of this period of upheaval in French society of the Belle Epoque.

In the domain of the French novel, the unique quality of Proust's achievement is evident from the fact that no subsequent novelist could afford to ignore the advances made by the author of the *Recherche,* especially—if not solely—in the areas of style and above all psychological analysis.

Of Proust's three contemporaries, only Gide sought to compete with him in the novel. In spite of such apparent links to the metaphorical as the accumulation of levels of meaning of the notion of counterfeiting in *Les Faux-Monnayeurs,* Gide remains far to the metonymic side of the spectrum by comparison with Proust: while problems of conventional religiosity such as the question of puritanism are dealt with in a work like *La Porte étroite,* it is only in the *Recherche* that the presence of the sacred becomes an ever-present, ubiquitous, almost palpable reality. Gide gives us an established professional novelist in Edouard, but Proust portrays a young man tormented by literature as by a sacred vocation, involving initiation, a dark night of the soul (years of despairing self-doubt), and ultimate confirmation and salvation. As a result, the whole conception of literature, life, and reality is transformed, and if Proust's somewhat mystical, almost pantheistic idealism is not for all tastes, Gide by comparison takes on the appearance of an amateur psychologist playing curious, even brilliant, but comparatively superficial games with the formal propensities of the genre.

III   *Metaphor and Metonymy*

New light can be thrown on Proust's achievement by reference to the historical, cultural, and intellectual context.

At the beginning of the twentieth century, French art had just passed through a severe crisis. With the slow expiration of romanticism visible in its later manifestations, a new orientation became almost inevitable. Romanticism had been something of a foreign transplant in any case, and the French sought to return to a truly French tradition, which—significantly enough—they saw best typified not in the classicism of Jean Racine, Charles Le Brun, and Jean-Baptiste Lully but in the rococo style of Marivaux, Antoine Watteau, and François Couperin. Such models provided the inspiration for representatives of all the arts, including Paul Verlaine, Renoir, and Claude Debussy—artists associated with the impressionist aesthetic.

What was the essential character of the rococo aesthetic to which the impressionists returned? In a word, it was metonymic. After the metaphorical thrust of the baroque (which, like the later romantic movement, was largely a foreign import in France), there was a shift toward the metonymic in all the arts. This movement is reflected in the weakening of the metaphorical signifiers, whether constitutive or thematic, in all the arts. The constitutive elements of poetry (verse and rhyme), painting (line and color), and music (melody and harmony) are metaphorical signifiers which have traditionally served to represent the artist's inner universe. When these weaken, other metaphorical levels (such as the thematic) also tend to lose their force or appeal; mythological, biblical, even merely historical subjects are abandoned in favor of contemporary realities. One has the impression of a general weakening of the creative drive—a loss of belief in the capacity of the artist to create an autonomous universe.

In the latter half of the seventeenth century, the swing from the metaphorical to the metonymic was reflected in the replacement of the baroque aesthetic, with its transcendental character, by the reductive rationalism characteristic of classicism. Peter Paul Rubens gives way to Nicolas Poussin and Lebrun, the great baroque sculptor Pierre Puget is excluded from Versailles, and the options represented by Gian Lorenzo Bernini in architecture and Francesco Cavalli in music are carefully considered during visits by these baroque artists to Paris and rejected in favor of Charles Perrault and

Lully. *Le Cid* is criticized for "irregularity" and the heroism of Pierre Corneille is displaced by the more reductive and realistic psychology of a Racine; the pastoral character of *L'Astrée* and the heroics of Madeleine de Scudéry give way to the unheroic historicism of *La Princesse de Clèves* with its stress on postmarital problems and a philosophy of prudence.

This movement toward the metonymic is completed n the rococo (beginning of the eighteenth century). In painting, line was fragmented and figures were given an apparently random distribution (Watteau, Jean-Honoré Fragonard), while color was diluted (François Boucher, Fragonard); in music, the melodic line was broken up and harmony reduced to a simplified base accompaniment. Both verse (*la mesure*) and rhyme were attacked as absurd—a movement further reflected in the truncation and fragmentation of artistic constructs. The heroic couplet was undermined by a mock-heroic tone (*The Rape of the Lock*), poems typically became brief and circumstantial, and when longer they gradually came to be diluted by admixtures of prose. Tragedy and farce (Corneille, Racine, Molière) were replaced by comedy of manners (Marivaux), and in the novel the historicism of *La Princesse de Clèves* is replaced by the realistic depiction of contemporary life, as in *La Vie de Marianne*. Novels were often left unfinished (*La Vie de Marianne*, *Le Paysan parvenu*, *Les Egarements du coeur et de l'esprit*), and fragmentary forms like the essay became extremely popular.

Just as classicism, in the seventeenth century, was a transitional phase in the movement from metaphorical baroque to metonymic rococo, so in the nineteenth century realism was a transitional phase between metaphorical romanticism, with its belief in the imagination as truly creative and in poetry as prophetic, and metonymic impressionism. Such is the true place of Gustave Courbet and Edouard Manet, of the Parnassian poets, Flaubert, and Zola, perhaps of Georges Bizet. Form, in all its studied completeness (metaphor of a whole, a being, a life) was still very important to Courbet and Manet, with their use of vivid colors and black and their use of clear outlines, to José-Maria de Hérédia with his predilection for the strict form of the sonnet, and to the authors of *Madame Bovary* and *Germinal*, although the departure from romanticism is evident in the effort to avoid sentimental effusions and in the fact that all these artists except the poets forsook the exotic to concentrate on contemporary realities.

The year 1874, which saw the first exhibition of the school of
painting soon christened "impressionist," also saw the "impressionist" program sketched out in Verlaine's *Art poétique*. What
was this program? In painting, the impressionists not only
fragmented the clear outline of Ingres as preserved by Manet but
they also diluted color by eliminating both black and all vivid
colors, reducing their palette to pastel shades only. They limited
themselves even more strictly than Courbet and Manet to the study
of contemporary life, returning explicitly to the rococo aesthetic,
which they studied in the Louvre in the paintings of Watteau,
Boucher, and Fragonard. Verlaine, whose taste for Watteau is evident in his *Fêtes galantes,* produces in his *Art poétique* a veritable
manifesto of impressionism. Previous manifestoes, such as those of
Théodore de Banville (1846) and Théophile Gautier (1857), had
echoed and developed further the plastic, Ingresque programme of
John Keats' *Ode on a Grecian Urn,* with its "brede/Of marble men
and maidens" and its explicit preference for the plastic over the
musical: "Heard melodies are sweet, but those unheard/Are
sweeter; therefore, ye soft pipes, play on;/Not to the sensual ear,
but, more endear'd,/Pipe to the spirit ditties of no tone." Verlaine,
on the contrary, calls for "De la musique avant toute
chose"—"Music before everything else." Whereas Gautier rejected
those media (typical of impressionism as of its ancestor, the rococo)
which lend themselves to rapidity of execution—the sculptor's clay,
the artist's crayons or watercolor—Verlaine proposes an aesthetic
which is very congenial to such vehicles with their fresh spontaneity
and their capacity for capturing the most evanescent of moods and
gestures. Not only is sculpture replaced by music, but within the
plastic arts color is replaced by shade (*la Nuance*), as within music
the sound of the flute is added to that of the horn. And finally, the
anagogic dimension represented in Gautier's poem by mythological
and religious references is completely eliminated by Verlaine, as are
the references to classical antiquity and the use of conventional
rhetoric.

Paradoxically, Verlaine's quest for what he calls "music"
expresses itself partly in the elimination of two of the chief sources
of music (in the sense of "aural pleasure") available to the poet,
namely, verse and rhyme. It is noteworthy that verse and rhyme,
the chief metaphorical signifiers of poetry, constitute means of in-
tegrating into literature both aural and visual effects (aural only, of
course, in the case of oral literature). This elimination, called for but

not illustrated in his *Art poétique*, eventually will find expression in Mallarmé's *Un coup de dés* and Lautréamont's *Chants de Maldoror*, which reject the visual and aural effects of regularity and repetition inscribed in traditional verse and rhyme—Lautréamont by filling the page to its margins and Mallarmé by fragmenting it with "randomly" distributed words adrift in a sea of open spaces.

In the novel, impressionism is represented by Edmond and Jules Goncourt with *Renée Mauperin*: emphasis on adjectives and abstract terms; broken rhythm; partial representation of people and things; fondness for suggestion and allusion; general fragmentation of form; simplified syntax, a sentence reduced to the essential, to a few outstanding elements abruptly juxtaposed; and the elimination of description or at least the shifting toward the middle of chapters of this slow, heavy element.[4]

Proust reflects the crisis of his age but seeks to resolve it. Metonymic in his choice of prose as the medium for his poetry, in his decision to depict contemporary reality, and in the highly syntagmatic character of much of his thought (for instance, the alignment of multiple causes, reasons, or motivations), he nevertheless manages to restore a central role to the metaphorical. Thus he continually has recourse to images—often very extended in dimensions—in which certain entities are compared to others of a different order, whether higher or lower, in such a manner as to effect transformations and metamorphoses often marked by transcendence and sometimes constituting veritable apotheoses. Metaphor is his weapon against time, with which he ever and anon leaves the ephemeral level of the profane to attain the changeless level of the sacred. The result is a blend of the metaphorical and the metonymic which provides a fitting harbinger of the brilliant new age of art and literature represented by the twentieth century.

IV *The Principle: Synthesis; the Instinct: Symbiosis*

It has been claimed that his psychology is indelibly marked by the atomism current at the end of the nineteenth century, but that is only half the truth. While he did indeed advance the microscopic analysis of sentiments and passions, he also managed to overcome the resulting fragmentation by means of a remarkable gift for synthesis.

This synthesis, which is a key taste and goal of our author, is represented on the instinctual level by the most extreme tendency to dissolve barriers and to unify intimately and indissolubly—an all-embracing aspiration to a veritable symbiosis. This fusion is achieved and represented by Proust in a manner and to a degree that is unique in the history of literature.

The very choice of first-person point of view has the effect of binding together the diverse elements of the narration and focussing on them a single source of perception, reflection, and interpretation. Beyond that, Proust creates a narrator whose central trait is a habit of symbiosis (in the form of dependence on the Mother) and a constant aspiration toward more complete interpenetration between himself and other persons, things, and places.

Proust, not twenty years younger than Sigmund Freud, goes beyond the novelists who preceded him by the deliberate introduction and the explicit study of a relatively new psychological dimension, that of the unconscious. Already discovered and exploited to some extent by the romantics, the unconscious now comes of age through the attempt to depict it by means of the psychopathology of language (the *lapsus linguae* which reveal a carefully dissimulated snobbery) and dreams. This emphasis further heightens unification, for the objective multiplicity of external reality is replaced by the much more relative multiplicity of the Self, with its foundation squarely based not on the Many but on the One. Thus it is that the multiplicity of love objects, which is stressed many times, is in fact subverted by the greater stress on the Stendhalian notion that desire precedes and creates them. Further, the function of desire is made so dependent on fictions (developed by the single Self) that it cannot survive confrontation with multifarious reality: desire depends on frustration, rivalry, or, at the very least, absence.

His characters are so complex that they appear to change totally from one period to another because of variations in the perspective, the angle of perception, the source, the quality, or the quantity of information available. Thus at least an appearance of inconsistency becomes an essential characteristic of psychological realism in character-portrayal. This again derives from the realistic depiction of growth and flux in the observing Self, the fiction of psychological consistency being largely a concomitant of the "objective," third-person narration so typical of the nineteenth century. Thus the very principle of variation in character-portrayal is a function not so much of diversity and fragmentation of reality but of organically continuous growth of the fusing principle, namely, the narrator-protagonist.

This principle of fusion also operates at the level of class structures: the protagonist and other bourgeois characters are continually disappointed to discover that the aristocracy has become so little different from the upper bourgeoisie: the myth of the nobility, dependent on an unknown but postulated and prestigious Otherness, is destroyed by familiarity. This destruction is eventually consummated by the social fusion triggered off by such developments as moral decadence and financial ruin, both traits rendering the aristocracy permeable to the bourgeoisie and even to some members of the working class. The prestigious myth of difference and impenetrability cannot survive except in dreams or in literature.

The narrator attributes a central role to the perception of relationships between things, and he even makes of this interrelationship (whether it is in the things perceived or rather in the perception of them) the foundation of metaphor and the basis of the literary vocation. This is further stressed by drawing together all the many elements of the *Recherche* as parts of a single life, his own, the revelation of whose unity is part of his realization of his source materials for his single great work destined to unify all his experiences and all his reflections.

For Proust, the goal of art must be to tear aside the veil of conventional signs, symbols, and associations which hides from us the original color and the irreplacable immediacy of our sense-impressions. This represents an abandonment to the irrational which reflects a skeptical attitude toward reason reminiscent of a Marivaux. Analytic reason is replaced by synthetic intuition—again a manifestation of the thrust toward unification.

Proust is the great healer, moving through metonymy to metaphor, through analysis to synthesis, to reconcile impressionism with symbolism, realism with idealism, reality with art, and man the dreamer with the reductive parameters of the human condition. Like Claudel (in *Le soulier de satin*), Gide (in *Les Faux-Monnayeurs*), and Valéry (in his *Cahiers*), he will seek to resolve the crisis reflected in impressionism (some of whose manifestations were often confused with symbolism) by reconciling lucidity with creativity, the rational with the intuitive, in an ambitious masterpiece devoted to an exploration and an explicit discussion of the parameters of literary creation and of the nature, conditions, and limitations of artistic creativity in general.

CHAPTER 11

Conclusion

PROUST criticism has only too often been marred by a failure to distinguish (as Proust himself insisted we must) between author, implied author, narrator, and protagonist. One result is a confused and illogical interpretation, even among the most recent and best Proust critics (such as Gilles Deleuze), of the Proustian achievement; the radically immanent approach, adumbrated by Proust himself and applied here (Chapters 1 - 9), has the advantage of being, on the contrary, rigorous and self-consistent. A second result is a certain passive text fetishism caused by the attribution of statements made by the fictional narrator of the *Recherche* to Proust himself, seen as brilliant and infallible; such an attitude is an insult to the intelligence, sensitivity, and superb craftsmanship of Proust, for both the fictional narrator on the one hand and Proust on the other are subject to the errors inherent in the subjectivity Proust has taught us to discern.

Perhaps the most serious defect in the narrator's view of reality lies in his skepticism and pessimism regarding human relations. These he appears to see as irrevocably marked by cowardice, masochism, sadism, dishonesty, inauthenticity, and general alienation. The total end result is a view of love as illusion and delusion and a general negation of happiness and an exaltation of suffering. The truth is that he sees it so because his attitude toward love is distorted by an apparently ineradicable immaturity and selfishness, and a tendency toward reification. Like Swann, he accepts venality in women as quite natural, and happily exploits it. A second serious defect derives from an aggravation of the first: it is the abusive development of this distorted, individual perspective—based on a partial and in fact abnormal set of experiences—into a set of conclusions of allegedly general validity. Thus happiness is virtually useless except to make unhappiness possible; love is always erroneous, an illness, inspired by obstacles, weakened by success (it

138

is rarely reciprocal), renewed by apparent indifference—we love because we must, certainly not because we are loved, and it moves us to harshness and dishonesty. It is perhaps needless to say that the universal validity of such propositions remains to be demonstrated.

These defects, of course, mar the narrator's character and view of the world, *not* Proust's creation, as we cannot assume either that the narrator is presenting Proust's ideas or that Proust intended him to be taken as penetrating, wise, and infallible. On the contrary, all that we know of Proust's extraordinary awareness of the conditions of his art lead us to think that he knew exactly what he was doing when he chose the first-person form and thus enabled himself to take full advantage of its function as a mode of profound ambiguity and subjectivity. Even disclaimers of his own as to any such intention cannot be taken at face value but are subject to caution.

What, then, is the positive side of the Proustian *Recherche?*

First, it resides in a brilliant rediscovery and illustration of the subtle first-person form which had virtually been lost sight of for over a century. First-person point of view had been a central characteristic of the eighteenth-century novel, from the confessional narrative of *Manon Lescaut* and single-author epistolary novels like *La Vie de Marianne* to multiple-author epistolary novels such as *Lettres persanes, La nouvelle Héloïse,* and *Les Liaison dangereuses.* This mode of fictional narration was exploited with particular brilliance in the rococo period,[2] possibly because of the suppression of personal, lyrical expression in poetry at that time. When lyric poetry came into its own again, in the romantic period, first-person narration fell into eclipse, Constant's *Adolphe* (1816) being the last example of note. To the extent that, unlike the third-person mode, the first person is virtually bound to the portrayal of the contemporary scene and in many ways reveals its own subjectivity, it may be considered reductive and in that sense metonymic.

Second, Proust has met the challenge of reconciling the two contrary poles of the human mind and its drives and aspirations, namely, the metaphorical and the metonymic. It is, of course, questionable whether such a reconciliation can continue to endure in a world apparently bent on the eventual elimination of the sacred and probably of the metaphorical (except of a superficial, largely technical kind); and if the metaphorical *is* to survive, it will probably do so in a form quite different from those known hitherto. Nevertheless, Proust's achievement here was a remarkable contribution for its time.

Finally, we owe to Proust an incredibly meticulous and perceptive evocation and exploration of what is in fact a case of abnormal psychology: only such an interpretation gives Proust his rightful place with contemporaries like Kafka as a specialist in the analysis of alienation and schizophrenia.[3] His work does not deal with such states in the concentrated and in a sense explicit (although of course symbolic) manner adopted by Kafka; but close textual study reveals many elements which can best be understood in the light of such a hypothesis. Of course, once we use the term "abnormal" we are adopting a "normative" perspective, and that is hard to justify in these days of relativity. Indeed, we should perhaps add to our view of "symbiotic schizophrenia" (derived from family behavior theory and transactional analysis) a cautionary reminder (inspired by the work of cultural historians like Michel Foucault) of the possible arbitrary nature of the categorization of various modes of behavior as "normal" or "abnormal." Thus symbiosis may be seen in a more positive light: by his insistence on mutual interpenetration (the cornerstone of his universe), Proust has opened our eyes to the possibility of an intimate communication not only with other people but even with plants, places, and things—a communion which we need if we are to accept our return, after death, to that eternal cosmic compost heap from which we originally sprang.

Plot Summary of
A la recherche du temps perdu
(Remembrance of Things Past)

I Du côté de chez Swann (Swann's Way)

The narrator evokes his childhood in Combray, the magic lantern in his bedroom, his mother's good-night kiss for which he hungered desperately. Recently the taste of a tea-cake soaked in lime tea reminded him of his Aunt Léonie and their life in Combray: the family used to go for long walks around the town, where he fell in love with the hawthorns and a little girl named Gilberte. The sight of three bell-towers caused him a strange pleasure, and he immediately wrote a description of them.

Charles Swann had fallen in love with Odette de Crécy, and joined for her sake the *salon* of the Verdurins. He associated with her a phrase from a sonata by the composer Vinteuil. Excluded from the salon as a snob because of his aristocratic connections, he received an anonymous letter accusing Odette of loose morals, of lesbianism, and even of prostitution. He later discovered that she had indeed been the mistress of his rival Forcheville. Swann and Odette ultimately marry nevertheless, and their daughter Gilberte becomes the protagonist's playmate.

II A l'ombre des jeunes filles en fleurs (Within a Budding Grove)

Swann and other characters appear in a new light. Ambassador Norpois lends his moral support to the literary ambitions of the protagonist. The latter hears the actress Berma for the first time and is disappointed. He makes friends with Gilberte, but she says her parents do not like him. Bloch and Cottard unintentionally gain access for him to Swann's house, where the first mention of Albertine occurs and where he meets Bergotte, who takes him to a brothel where he sees the prostitute Rachel. There follow frequent visits to the Swanns', but he eventually arrives at the conviction that

141

love destroys happiness, and he eventually loses contact with Gilberte.

The protagonist leaves with his grandmother for Balbec, where they stay at the Grand Hotel. The narrator describes Aimé, the headwaiter, satirizes the snobbery of provincial notables, and evokes Mlle de Stermaria as the quintessence of romantic Brittany. On a trip through the countryside, he sees near Hudimesnil three trees which move him by their suggestion of a secret message. He makes friends with Robert de Saint-Loup, and encounters Robert's Uncle M. de Charlus, and the Bloch family. He falls in love with a band of girls, and especially one: Albertine. He gets to know them through Elstir, whose studio he visits. His preference vacillates between Andrée, Gisèle, and Albertine, but he finally prefers Albertine, who encourages him but refuses to allow him to kiss her.

III   Le Côté de Guermantes (The Guermantes Way)

In Paris, the protagonist's family moves into an apartment attached to the *hôtel* des Guermantes. He visits the Guermantes' box at the Opéra, an experience which merely confirms his conviction of the unreality of the Guermantes and the denizens of the Faubourg Saint-Germain. He becomes obsessed with the duchess, and visits Saint-Loup at his barracks. The Dreyfus case breaks out; his maternal grandmother becomes ill; Saint-Loup's adored mistress turns out to be the prostitute Rachel. High society opens its doors to the protagonist, who finds Robert's aunt, Oriane de Guermantes, very cordial; he is the object of advances from M. de Charlus. The Dreyfus case continues to preoccupy society. The protagonist's grandmother suffers a serious attack.

After a grave illness, his grandmother dies. Albertine visits him, and he recovers from his obsession with the duchess. He has a rendezvous with Mlle de Stermaria, but she is finally unable to come. Invited to dinner at the Guermantes', he notes the celebrated wit of Oriane but suffers a general disappointment at the level of conversation. He is taken home by Charlus. Swann, who is a supporter of Dreyfus, falls seriously ill.

IV   Sodome et Gomorrhe (Cities of the Plain)

The protagonist observes an encounter between M. de Charlus and Jupien, who turn out to be both homosexuals. A brilliant evening at the Princesse de Guermantes' brings together Charlus, Vaugoubert, and Bréauté, and various mistresses old and new of the duke, and is the occasion of a significant conversation between the prince and Swann. The protagonist begins to feel the need for Albertine. Meanwhile, Odette's *salon* gradually achieves social success. At Balbec, the protagonist has vivid and painful memories of his grandmother, accompanied by distress and remorse. He sees Albertine.

His relationship with Albertine develops; he watches her dancing with Andrée; Albertine resembles Odette from certain points of view. Lesbian scandals shake the hotel. Charlus takes up with a young violinist named Morel, whom he accompanies to evenings at the Verdurins' rented villa, La Raspelière. Charlus is arrogant, but he is treated harshly by Morel, who also shows other signs of harshness and lack of scruples; the prince becomes a rival of Charlus for Morel. The protagonist decides not to marry Albertine.

Albertine turns out to be a friend of Mlle de Vinteuil; jealous again, the protagonist decides to marry Albertine after all.

V   La Prisonnière (The Captive)

The protagonist sends to *Le Figaro* as an article a touched-up version of his evocation of the three bell-towers of Martinville. Albertine comes to live with the protagonist in Paris, where she grows intellectually as she declines physically. He has Andrée chaperone her on outings, and gets advice from the duchess on Albertine's wardrobe. At this point we are given portraits of several homosexuals: Jupien, Charlus, Morel; Jupien's niece falls in love with Morel, who later treats her cruelly. Albertine avoids his good-night kiss, and the protagonist becomes suspicious of her, perhaps because he himself is strongly attracted to others (for instance, working-girls he sees); his feelings toward her oscillate from desire to boredom. Meanwhile, Bergotte dies at a Ver Meer exhibition. Albertine lies constantly, and he decides to break with her. There are signs of moral decline in Charlus; he organizes an evening for Morel at the Verdurins', and those he invites are insolent toward the Verdurins, who get Morel to break with Charlus. The protagonist reflects on the music of Vinteuil, which he gets Albertine to play for him. He suggests to Albertine that they separate; she again avoids his good-night kiss, and he finally decides definitely to leave her, only to discover that she has already left him.

VI   La Fugitive (The Sweet Cheat Gone)

The protagonist suffers at Albertine's departure, and wants to bring her back and marry her. He invites Andrée to stay with him, and sends Saint-Loup to find Albertine, who complains of this in a letter. Her aunt informs him of Albertine's death in an accident. He sends Aimé to enquire about her past activities at Balbec, and is informed of Albertine's promiscuous lesbianism. He encounters Gilberte, now Mlle de Forcheville (Swann dead, Odette has married his rival, who has adopted his daughter). The protagonist's article on the three bell-towers is published in *Le Figaro*. Andrée admits to lesbian relations with Albertine, who had also teamed up with Morel to corrupt young girls. Later, the protagonist travels with his mother to Venice, where he receives a telegram apparently from Albertine; in reality it is from Gilberte, engaged to Saint-Loup. Once married to Gilberte, Saint-Loup deceives her with Morel.

VII   Le Temps retrouvé (The Past Recaptured)

The protagonist has several conversations with Gilberte. World War I breaks out, revealing the cowardice of Morel and the bravery of Saint-Loup. Charlus, who is pro-German, is attacked in the press by Morel, whom he threatens to kill. Charlus establishes and regularly visits a special brothel (for masochists and such) run by Jupien. Saint-Loup dies; Morel is arrested for desertion and sent to the front, where he shows courage. Years later, the protagonist returns to Paris, and there encounters Charlus and Jupien. He steps on uneven paving-stones, experiences a pleasure comparable to that caused by the tea-soaked *madeleine;* also has other similar experiences, associated with involuntary memory, during which the present coincides with the past to liberate an atemporal essence of things. He develops the theory that pain and jealousy are valuable in the development of the mind. The dramatic effect of age on old acquaintances is indicated, together with astonishing social changes: not only has the Duc de Guermantes begun a liaison with Odette, but Mme Verdurin has become Princesse de Guermantes. The protagonist resolves to devote the remainder of his life to a literary work on the theme of Time.

Notes and References

Preface

1. The French title means literally "In Search of Past Time": the French expression "A la recherche de . . ." is more active than the title of the standard English translation—the term "Remembrance" corresponds rather to the French term "Souvenir." The work will be referred to henceforth as "the *Recherche*." The following abbreviations are used: *SW, Swann's Way (Du côté de chez Swann); WBG, Within a Budding Grove (A l'ombre des jeunes filles en fleurs); GW, The Guermantes Way (Le Côté de Guermantes); CP, Cities of the Plain (Sodome et Gomorrhe); C, The Captive (La Prisonnière); SCG, The Sweet Cheat Gone (La Fugitive); PR, The Past Recaptured (Le Temps retrouvé); Pl*, Pléïade edition.

Chapter One

1. It may seem unnecessary to belabor this point since the work of scholars like Marcel Muller's *Les Voix narratives dans la "Recherche du temps perdu"* (Genève: Droz, 1965). The truth is, however, that some of the best and most recent critics (for example, Deleuze, Mehlmann) neglect this essential aspect of the work, thus rendering their analysis superficial and their conclusions fragile. If Muller has failed to prevent such abuses, it may be because his own position is in fact not rigorously immanent: he refuses to see the Protagonist as really fictitious (p. 13), and appears to espouse Cocking's pointless speculations as to Proust's "intentions" (p. 20 and n. 31).

2. *SCG*, 47 (*Pl*, III, 450).
3. *SW*, 520 - 21 (*Pl*, I, 403 - 04).
4. *C*, 91 (*Pl*, III, 75).
5. *C*, 207 (*Pl*, III, 157).
6. *GW*, II, 171 (*Pl*, II, 432).
7. *SCG*, 309 (*Pl*, III, 641).
8. *PR*, 264 (*Pl*, III, 929).
9. *C*, 427 (*Pl*, III, 316).
10. *C*, 52 (*Pl*, III, 46).
11. *C*, 475 (*Pl*, III, 348).
12. *C*, 317 (*Pl*, III, 235).
13. *CP*, I, 71 - 72 (*Pl*, II, 651 - 52).
14. *C*, 241 (*Pl*, III, 181).
15. *C*, 441 (*Pl*, III, 325).

16. *C*, 463 (*Pl*, III, 338).

17. *C*, 526 (*Pl*, III, 386).

18. *C*, 289 (*Pl*, III, 214).

19. *SCG*, 273 (*Pl*, III, 615).

20. *SCG*, 370 (*Pl*, III, 688).

21. *SW*, 202 (*Pl*, I, 157).

22. *GW*, I, 83 - 84 (*Pl*, II, 67).

23. *SCG*, 137 (*Pl*, III, 515).

24. *CP*, II, 268 - 69, (*Pl*, II, 1049).

25. *PR*, 199, 201 (*Pl*, III, 958, 960).

26. *WBG*, I, 341 (*Pl*, I, 665).

27. *CP*, II, 324 (*Pl*, II, 1088).

28. *C*, 287 - 88 (*Pl*, III, 213).

29. *C*, 389 (*Pl*, III, 288).

30. *SCG*, 115 (*Pl*, III, 499). See *CP*, I, 208; *SCG*, 260 - 61; *PR*, 118, 123, 134, 291 - 92, 340 - 41 (*Pl*, II, 750; III, 605 - 6, 804, 808, 818, 953 - 54, 995 - 96).

31. *SW*, 11 - 12 (*Pl*, I, 10).

32. *SW*, 29 - 30 (*Pl*, I, 25 - 26).

33. *SW*, 29 (*Pl*, I, 25).

34. *CP*, II, 1 (*Pl*, II, 854).

35. *CP*, II, 306 (*Pl*, II, 1076).

36. *CP*, II, 303 - 4 (*Pl*, II, 1074).

37. *CP*, II, 139 - 40 (*Pl*, II, 955).

38. *CP*, II, 64 (*Pl*, II, 900).

39. *GW*, II, 279 (*Pl*, II, 521). See *SW*, 434 - 35, 442 (*Pl*, I, 335, 341).

40. *GW*, II, 164 - 65 (*Pl*, II, 427 - 28).

41. *SW*, 113 (*Pl*, I, 90).

42. *GW*, II, 340 (*Pl*, II, 556).

43. *CP*, II, 139 (*Pl*, II, 955).

44. *GW*, I, 334 - 36 (*Pl*, II, 245 - 46). See *PR*, 92 (*Pl*, III, 782).

45. *CP*, I, 283 (*Pl*, II, 803).

46. *GW*, II, 124 (*Pl*, II, 398).

47. *C*, 231 (*Pl*, III, 174).

48. *WBG*, II, 212 (*Pl*, I, 853).

49. *GW*, II, 180 (*Pl*, II, 439).

50. *WBG*, II, 212 (*Pl*, I, 853).

51. *C*, 393 (*Pl*, III, 291).

52. *CP*, I, 265 (*Pl*, II, 789).

53. *C*, 123 (*Pl*, III, 97).

54. *C*, 463 (*Pl*, III, 338).

55. *C*, 466 (*Pl*, III, 340 - 41).

56. *SCG*, 183 (*Pl*, III, 549).

57. *SCG*, 313 (*Pl*, III, 643).

58. *SCG*, 268 (*Pl*, III, 611).

59. *GW*, II, 77 (*Pl*, II, 365).
60. *SCG*, 113 (*Pl*, III, 498).
61. Passage missing from Scott-Moncrieff but included in the Pléïade edition, III, 206 - 7.
62. *PR*, 240 - 41 (*Pl*, III, 909).

Chapter Two

1. *SW*, 1 (*Pl*, I, 3).
2. *SW*, 4 (*Pl*, I, 5).
3. *GW*, I, 112 (*Pl*, II, 88).
4. *WBG*, II, 165 - 66 (*Pl*, I, 819 - 20).
5. *SW*, 490 (*Pl*, I, 378).
6. *SW*, 491 (*Pl*, I, 379).
7. *SW*, 521 (*Pl*, I, 404).
8. *PR*, 211 (*Pl*, III, 884).
9. *SCG*, 23 (*Pl*, III, 434). See *WBG*, I, 102 (*Pl*, I, 500).
10. *G.W.* I, 408 (*Pl*, II, 298).
11. *WBG*, II, 288 (*Pl*, I, 907).
12. *WBG*, I, 330 (*Pl*, I, 658).
13. *WBG*, II, 340 (*Pl*, I, 943).
14. *WBG*, II, 212 (*Pl*, I, 853).
15. *GW*, I, 80 (*Pl*, II, 65).
16. *WBG*, II, 259 (*Pl*, I, 886).
17. *WBG*, II, 287 (*Pl*, I, 906 - 7).
18. *WBG*, I, 201 (*Pl*, I, 569).
19. *WBG*, II, 234 (*Pl*, I, 869).
20. *WBG*, II, 258 (*Pl*, I, 886).
21. *WBG*, II, 259 (*Pl*, I, 886).
22. *WBG*, II, 61 (*Pl*, I, 746).
23. *WBG*, II, 212 (*Pl*, I, 853).
24. Ibid.
25. Ibid.
26. *SCG*, 45 (*Pl*, III, 449).
27. *CP*, II, 6 (*Pl*, II, 858).
28. *CP*, II, 122 (*Pl*, II, 942).
29. *C*, 33 (*Pl*, III, 32).
30. *SCG.*, 262 (*Pl*, III, 606).
31. Passage missing from Scott-Moncrieff but included in the Pléïade edition, III, 708 n.
32. *C*, 488 (*Pl*, III, 358).
33. *PR*, 237 (*Pl*, III, 905 - 6).
34. *PR*, 240 (*Pl*, III, 908).
35. *PR*, 226 - 27 (*Pl*, III, 897).
36. *SW*, 13 (*Pl*, I, 12).

37. *C*, 394 (*Pl*, III, 291).
38. *C*, 225 - 26 (*Pl*, III, 170).
39. *GW*, I, 82 (*Pl*, II, 66).
40. *C*, 96 (*Pl*, III, 78).
41. *C*, 97 (*Pl*, III, 79). See *C*, 484 (*Pl*, III, 354).
42. *WBG*, II, 339 (*Pl*, I, 943).
43. *WBG*, II, 269 (*Pl*, I, 893 - 94).
44. *WBG*, II, 299 (*Pl*, I, 914).
45. *C*, 186 (*Pl*, III, 142). See *CP*, II, 212 (*Pl*, II, 1008): Morel.
46. *CP*, II, 218 (*Pl*, II, 1013).
47. *P.R*, 310 (*Pl*, III, 968).
48. *SW*, 281 (*Pl*, I, 218).

Chapter Three

1. *SW*, 113 (*Pl*, I, 91).
2. *GW*, I, 186 - 87 (*Pl*, II, 140).
3. *WBG*, I, 342 (*Pl*, I, 666).
4. *WBG*, I, 343 (*Pl*, I, 667).
5. *GW*, I, 186 - 87 (*Pl*, II, 140).
6. *SCG*, 194 (*Pl*, III, 557).
7. *CP*, I, 277 (*Pl*, II, 798).
8. *GW*, I, 209 (*Pl*, II, 156).
9. *SCG*, 56 (*Pl*, III, 457).
10. *CP*, I, 327 (*Pl*, II, 835).
11. *SCG*, 111 (*Pl*, III, 496).
12. *SCG*, 124 (*Pl*, III, 506).
13. *C*, 144 (*Pl*, III, 111).
14. *SCG*, 267 - 68 (*Pl*, III, 610 - 11).
15. *SW*, 34 (*Pl*, I, 28 - 29).
16. *GW*, II, 73 (*Pl*, II, 363).
17. *WBG*, II, 219 (*Pl*, I, 858).
18. *PR*, 201 (*Pl*, III, 875).
19. *GW*, I, 233 (*Pl*, II, 173).
20. *WBG*, II, 218 - 219 (*Pl*, I, 858).
21. *GW*, I, 164 (*Pl*, II, 124).
22. *SW*, 46 - 47 (*Pl*, I, 38 - 39).
23. "From the standpoint of triangles, the 'parental we-ness' presents the child with a locked-in 'two-against-one' situation which provides no emotional flexibility unless he can somehow manage to force a rift in the other side of the triangle" ([Murray Bowen], "Toward the Differentiation of a Self in One's Own Family," *Family Interaction: A Dialogue Between Family Researchers and Family Therapists*, ed. J. L. Framo [New York: Springer, 1972], p. 143).
24. "The three areas in which 'undifferentiation' is absorbed in a

nuclear family are marital conflict, sickness or dysfunction in a spouse, and projection to one or more children" (ibid., p. 149).

25. *PR*, 214 - 15 (*Pl*, III, 886 - 87). See *PR*, 399 - 400 (*Pl*, III, 1044).

26. *WBG*, I, 315 - 16 (*Pl*, I, 648).

27. *WBG*, II, 117, 61 (*Pl*, I, 786, 746).

28. *WBG*, I, 344 (*Pl*, I, 668).

29. *SCG*, 288 (*Pl*, III, 624).

30. For example, *SCG*, 319 - 24 (*Pl*, III, 652 - 55).

31. *C*, 527 (*Pl*, III, 387).

32. *SW*, 140 - 41 (*Pl*, I, 111).

33. *WBG*, I, 379; *GW*, I, 197; *SCG*, 217 (*Pl*, I, 692; II, 147; III, 573).

34. *SCG*, 208 (*Pl*, III, 567).

35. *C*, 9 (*Pl*, III, 15).

36. *GW*, I, 15 (*Pl*, II, 19).

37. *SW*, 155 (*Pl*, I, 122).

38. *SW*, 155 - 56 (*Pl*, I, 122 - 23).

39. *SW*, 156 (*Pl*, I, 123).

40. Murray Bowen, p. 140.

41. *SW*, 198 (*Pl*, I, 154). See *GW*, I, 20 (*Pl*, II, 22).

42. *SW*, 242 (*Pl*, I, 188).

43. " . . . much 'triangling' took place at coffee breaks, social gatherings, and bull sessions in which the 'understanding' ones would 'analyse' and talk about those who were not present. The mechanism conveys 'We understand each other perfectly (the togetherness side of the triangle). We are in agreement about that pathological third person' " (Murray Bowen, p. 131).

44. *SW*, 244 (*Pl*, I, 189).

45. "A reasonably differentiated person is capable of genuine concern for others without expecting something in return, but the togetherness forces treat differentiation as selfish and hostile" (Murray Bowen, p. 140).

46. *SW*, 245 (*Pl*, I, 190).

47. "Gossip is one of the principal mechanisms for 'triangling' another into the emotional field between two people" (Murray Bowen, p. 130).

48. *Capitalisme et schizophrénie: L'anti-Oedipe* (Paris: Minuit, 1972).

49. *GW*, II, 74 - 77 (*Pl*, II, 363 - 65).

50. Deleuze et Guattari, p. 82.

51. M.-A. Séchehaye, *Journal d'une schizophrène* (Paris: Presses Universitaires de France, 1950).

52. *C*, 5 (*Pl*, III, 12). See *C*, 1 (*Pl*, III, 9).

53. *C*, 5 (*Pl*, III, 12).

54. Murray Bowen, p. 115.

55. Ibid., pp. 117 - 18, 122.

56. Ibid., pp. 118 - 19.

57. Ibid., p. 120.

58. Ibid., p. 130.

Chapter Four

1. That money ultimately counts even more than social class is proven by the marriage of the ruined Prince de Guermantes with Mme Verdurin, who comes from a bourgeois family that is immensely wealthy but totally "obscure."
2. *C*, 556 (*Pl*, III, 408).
3. *SCG*, 66 (*Pl*, III, 464).
4. *SCG*, 125 (*Pl*, III, 506 - 7).
5. Odette, *SCG*, 218 - 19 (*Pl*, III, 574); Gilberte, *SCG*, 325, 335 - 36 (*Pl*, III, 656, 661 n.); Jupien's niece, *SCG*, 328 - 29 (*Pl*, III, 658); Mme Verdurin, *PR*, 293 (*Pl*, III, 955); also *PR*, 310 - 11 (*Pl*, III, 968 - 69), etc.
6. *C*, 98 (*Pl*, III, 79).
7. *C*, 59 (*Pl*, III, 51).
8. *C*, 117 (*Pl*, III, 93).
9. *WBG*, II, 92 (*Pl*, I, 769).
10. *C*, 14 (*Pl*, III, 18).
11. The narrator denies the preference for intellectual pleasures attributed to the protagonist by Bergotte: *WBG*, I, 202 (*Pl*, I, 569 - 70). The little musical phrase by Vinteuil enables Swann also to transcend intellectual pleasures by means of others—*SW*, 307 (*Pl*, I, 237).
12. *GW*, II, 67 (*Pl*, II, 358).
13. *WBG*, II, 163 - 64 (*Pl*, I, 818). See *C*, 186 - 87 (*Pl*, III, 142).
14. *C*, 168 (*Pl*, III, 129).
15. *GW*, I, 139 - 40 (*Pl*, II, 106 n.).
16. *CP*, II, 373 - 74 (*Pl*, II, 1123).
17. *WBG*, II, 61 (*Pl*, I, 746).
18. *SW*, 220 - 21; *GW*, I, 8, 278, 285 (*Pl*, I, 171 - 72; II, 14, 204, 209).
19. *WBG*, 298 - 99 (*Pl*, I, 636).
20. *SW*, 202 (*Pl*, I, 157).
21. *PR*, 335 (*Pl*, III, 989 - 90). See *SW*, 221 (*Pl*, I, 172): Oriane.
22. *WBG*, I, 375 - 76 (*Pl*, I, 689).
23. *SW*, 220 - 21 (*Pl*, I, 171).
24. *SW*, 194 (*Pl*, I, 151).
25. *WBG*, I, 272 (*Pl*, I, 618).

Chapter Five

1. *WBG*, I, 301 (*Pl*, I, 637).
2. *PR*, 81 (*Pl*, III, 771).
3. *WBG*, I, 234 (*Pl*, I, 591).
4. *C*, 78 (*Pl*, III, 64 - 65).
5. *WBG*, I, 350 (*Pl*, I, 671).
6. *PR*, 244 (*Pl*, III, 912).
7. *C*, 255 (*Pl*, III, 191).
8. *GW*, I, 102 (*Pl*, II, 80 - 81).

9. *SW*, 60 - 62 (*Pl*, I, 49 - 50).
10. *GW*, I, 93 (*Pl*, II, 74).
11. Ibid.
12. *SW*, 103 (*Pl*, I, 83).
13. *WBG*, I, 351 - 52 (*Pl*, I, 673).
14. *PR*, 8 (*Pl*, III, 703).
15. *GW*, I, 289 (*Pl*, II, 212).
16. *SW*, 1 (*Pl*, I, 3).
17. *SCG*, 67 (*Pl*, III, 464 - 65).
18. *WBG*, I, 342 - 43 (*Pl*, I, 666 - 67).
19. *GW*, I, 2 (*Pl*, II, 10).
20. *GW*, I, 104 - 5 (*Pl*, II, 82).
21. *GW*, I, 107 (*Pl*, II, 84). See *GW*, I, 111 (*Pl*, II, 87).
22. *SCG*, 86 (*Pl*, III, 478).
23. *SW*, 10 (*Pl*, I, 10).
24. *CP*, II, 248 - 49 (*Pl*, II, 1035). Many passages suggest the interpenetration or even the undifferentiation of earth and sea, even air.
25. *SW*, 79 (*Pl*, I, 64).
26. *GW*, I, 125 (*Pl*, II, 97).
27. *GW*, II, 153 (*Pl*, II, 419).
28. *CP*, II, 38 (*Pl*, II, 881).
29. *CP*, I, 47 (*Pl*, II, 633).
30. *GW*, II, 361 - 62 (*Pl*, II, 572).
31. *SW*, 376 (*Pl*, I, 290). See *CP*, II, 268 - 69 (*Pl*, II, 1049), where the same image is applied to Charlus.
32. *GW*, I, 49 (*Pl*, II, 43).
33. *GW*, I, 125 (*Pl*, II, 97).
34. *WBG*, I, 363 - 64 (*Pl*, I, 681).
35. *WBG*, II, 156 (*Pl*, I, 813).
36. *SCG*, 145 (*Pl*, III, 521).
37. *GW*, I, 41 - 42 (*Pl*, II, 38).
38. *GW*, I, 45 (*Pl*, II, 40).
39. *SW*, 146 (*Pl*, I, 115).
40. *SW*, 237 (*Pl*, I, 184).
41. *WBG*, I, 240 (*Pl*, I, 595).
42. *C*, 273 (*Pl*, III, 203).

Chapter Six

1. ". . . obscure impressions had sometimes, even as far back as Combray along the Guermantes way, engaged my thoughts after the manner of those subjective recollections, but these others concealed within themselves, not a sensation of bygone days, but a new truth" (PR, 204 [*Pl*, III, 878]).
2. *SW*, 238 (*Pl*, I, 185).

3. *WBG*, II, 20 - 23 (*Pl*, I, 717 - 19).
4. *SW*, 231 - 34 (*Pl*, I, 180 - 82).
5. *SW*, 229 (*Pl*, I, 178).
6. *PR*, 196 - 201 (*Pl*, III, 871 - 75).
7. G. Deleuze, *Proust et les signes* (Paris: Presses Universitaires de France, 1971), pp. 17, 18, etc.
8. *WBG*, I, 330 - 31 (*Pl*, I, 658 - 59); *CP*, I, 310 - 11 (*Pl*, II, 822 - 23); *PR*, 1 (*Pl*, III, 698).
9. *PR*, 71 (*Pl*, III, 762 - 63).
10. *PR*, 177 - 78, 189 (*Pl*, III, 855, 865).
11. *GW*, I, 215 - 16 (*Pl*, II, 160 - 61).
12. Three tall pear-trees near where Rachel lives perform the function of maypoles hung with streamers: they are "gallantly beflagged with white satin", as though for some local civic festival (*G.W.I.*, 208 [*Pl.*, II, 155]). Other triads, not of visible objects, are not relevant.
13. *GW*, II, 123; *C*, 6; *SCG*, 209 - 15, 231, 240 - 42 (*Pl*, II, 397; III, 12 - 13, 567 - 72, 583, 589 - 91).
14. *SW*, 231 (*Pl*, I, 180).
15. *SW*, 238 (*Pl*, I, 185).
16. *WBG*, II, 20 (*Pl*, I, 717).
17. *SW*, 231 - 32 (*Pl*, I, 180).
18. *WBG*, II, 20 (*Pl*, I, 717).
19. Ibid.
20. *SW*, 232 - 33 (*Pl*, I, 181).
21. In the case of the trees, the narrator's text contains such a description, but it was not executed at the time of the observation itself, as was that of the bell-towers.
22. *SW*, 234 (*Pl*, I, 182); my italics.
23. *PR*, 205 (*Pl*, III, 878 - 79); my italics. See *PR*, 190 (*Pl*, III, 866).
24. "Where I had sought great laws, they called me one who grubs for petty details" (*PR*, 394 [*Pl*, III, 1041]).
25. *SW*, 232 (*Pl*, I, 181 - 82).
26. Ibid.
27. *WBG*, II, 22 - 23 (*Pl*, I, 719).
28. "I have wondered many times, in clinical practice, if such a thing as a dyad really exists. For example, in a mother-child schizophrenic relationship, one wonders if there is not always a third party present. It is difficult to conceive that two people can be related so intensely in a symbiotic way without having to differentiate themselves, as a unit, from a third party. The third party operates as a differentiating factor which solidifies and reassures the existence of the dyad" (Eli Rubinstein, in *Family Interaction*, p. 167).
29. *S.W.*, 238 (Pl, I, 185).
30. *SCG*, 319 (*Pl*, III, 652). "From the standpoint of triangles, the 'parental we-ness' presents the child with a locked-in 'two against one'

situation which provides no emotional flexibility unless he can somehow manage to force a rift in the other side of the traingle" (Murray Bowen, p. 143).

31. *PR*, 397 - 402 (*Pl*, III, 1044 - 1048).

32. *PR*, 401 (*Pl*, III, 1048).

33. My thesis that the two bell-towers of Martinville represent the unstable binary grouping of Mother and Son is further supported by a passage in *Contre Sainte-Beuve* evoking the two bell-towers of Chartres: "J'allai vers eux comme vers le moment où il faudrait dire adieu à maman, sentir mon coeur s'ébranler dans ma poitrine, se détacher de moi pour la suivre et revenir seul!" (*p.* 291).

Chapter Seven

1. *PR*, 9 - 10 (*Pl*, III, 705).

2. *GW*, II, 284 (*Pl*, II, 515).

3. *SW*, 180 - 181 (*Pl*, I, 141).

4. *WBG*, I, 299 (*Pl*, I, 636).

5. *GW*, I, 55 (*Pl*, II, 47).

6. *GW*, I, 190 (*Pl*, II, 142).

7. *WBG*, II, 141 (*Pl*, I, 802).

8. *PR*, 46 (*Pl*, III, 737).

9. *SW*, 3 (*Pl*, I, 5). See *C*, 102 (*Pl*, III, 82): "To lie still in bed was to let the lights and shadows play around me as round a tree-trunk."

10. *GW*, I, 191 (*Pl*, II, 143).

11. *GW*, I, 12 (*Pl*, II, 17). See *WBG*, II, 235 (*Pl*, I, 869).

12. *SCG*, 86 - 87 (*Pl*, III, 479).

13. *GW*, II, 280 (*Pl*, II, 512).

14. *CP*, II, 380 - 81 (*Pl*, II, 1128).

15. *SW*, 14 - 15 (*Pl*, I, 14).

16. *PR*, 400 (*Pl*, III, 1046).

17. *C*, 2 (*Pl*, III, 10). The sacred character of these kisses and the link with those of the Mother are even more clearly expressed in the following passage: "When it was Albertine's turn to bid me good-night, kissing me on either side of my throat, her hair caressed me like a wing of softly bristling feathers. Incomparable as were these two kisses of peace, Albertine slipped into my mouth, making me the gift of her tongue, like a gift of the Holy Spirit, conveyed to me a viaticum, left me with a provision of tranquility almost as precious as when my mother in the evening at Combray used to lay her lips upon my brow" (*C*, 95 - 96 [*Pl*, III, 1070—note to III, 78]). The assimilation of Albertine's kiss to his mother's occurs at least four other times.

18. There appears to be an assimilation of various modes of swallowing, the object being the *madeleine* (eating), the tongue (kissing), etc. The mouth is the apparent referent for perspectives on the bell (lips, tongue)

and so on. The anthropophagous implications of the labial kiss are stressed by Paul d'Enjoy, Robert Briffault, and Bronislaw Malinowski: primitive kissing involves not only saliva but also blood. See N. J. Perella, *The Kiss Sacred and Profane* (Berkeley: University of Calfornia Press, 1969).

19. *C*, 276 (*Pl*, III, 205).

20. He also aspires to drink Albertine's whole being through her eyes (*WBG*, II, 131 [*Pl*, I, 795]). Moreover, eyes and cheeks are assimilated in two curious phrases, in which he refers to cheeks "shining like eyes" (*C*, 92 [*Pl*, III, 75]), and to sensual cheeks which have "a look whose meaning it was difficult to grasp" (*SCG*, 118 [*Pl*, III, 502]).

21. *SW*, 2 (*Pl*, I, 4).

22. He says of his grandmother: "When I felt my mouth glued to her cheeks, to her brows, I drew from them something so beneficial, so nourishing, that I lay in her arms as motionless, as solemn, as calmly gluttonous as a babe at the breast" (*WBG*, I, 344 - 45 [*Pl*, I, 668]).

23. *SW*, 32 (*Pl*, I, 27).

24. *CP*, I, 273 (*Pl*, II, 795).

25. *GW*, II, 74 - 75 (*Pl*, II, 364).

26. *CP*, I, 326 - 27 (*Pl*, II, 834 - 35).

27. *SCG*, 113 (*Pl*, III, 497 - 98).

28. See above, Ch. 3, III.

29. *CP*, I, 184 (*Pl*, II, 733).

30. *SW*, 10 - 11 (*Pl*, I, 10).

31. *WBG*, I, 300 - 301 (*Pl*, I, 637).

32. *GW*, I, 85 (*Pl*, II, 68).

33. *GW*, I, 209, 210 (*Pl*, II, 157, 158).

34. *CP*, I, 287, 290 (*Pl*, II, 806, 808).

35. *C*, 527 (*Pl*, III, 387); *GW*, II, 77 (*Pl*, II, 365).

36. *C*, 330 (*Pl*, III, 244); *C*, 336 (*Pl*, III, 248).

37. *GW*, II, 32 (*Pl*, II, 334). See *CP*, II, 381 (*Pl*, II, 1129).

38. *WBG*, II, 314 (*Pl*, I, 925).

39. *WBG*, II, 325 (*Pl*, I, 933).

40. The reader may consult in this connection M. Guiomar, *Principes d'une esthétique de la mort* (Paris: Corti, 1967). Incredibly enough, Guiomar does not mention Proust.

41. *SW*, 2 - 4, 28, 60 (*Pl*, I, 3 - 5, 24, 49).

42. *SW*, 33 (*Pl*, I, 28).

43. *WBG*, II, 212 (*Pl*, I, 853).

44. *WBG*, I, 343 (*Pl*, I, 667).

45. *GW*, I, 95 (*Pl*, II, 75).

46. *SW*, 184 (*Pl*, I, 144).

47. *GW*, I, 94 - 96 (*Pl*, II, 75 - 76).

48. *GW*, I, 117 (*Pl*, II, 91).

49. *GW*, I, 178 (*Pl*, II, 134).

50. *SW*, 4, 28 (*Pl*, I, 5, 24).

51. *SW*, 161 (*Pl*, I, 127).
52. *SW*, 60 (*Pl*, I, 49).
53. *SW*, 203 (*Pl*, I, 158).
54. *PR*, 237 (*Pl*, III, 906).
55. *PR*, 241 (*Pl*, II, 909).
56. *CP*, I, 258 - 59 (*Pl*, II, 785).
57. *CP*, II, 362 - 63 (*Pl*, II, 1115).
58. Ibid.
59. *SW*, 4 (*Pl*, I, 5).
60. *SW*, I, 145 (*Pl*, I, 115).
61. *WBG*, II, 313 (*Pl*, I, 924).

Chapter Eight

1. *SW*, 54 - 58, 63 - 64, 239, (*Pl*, 44 - 48, 52, 186).
2. *SW*, 82 (*Pl*, I, 67).
3. *PR*, 191 (*Pl*, III, 866).
4. *PR*, 204 (*Pl*, III, 878).
5. *PR*, 191 - 93, 199 - 200 (*Pl*, III, 866 - 69, 874).
6. *PR*, 206 (*Pl*, III, 880).
7. *WBG*, I, 75 - 76 (*Pl*, I, 482 - 83).
8. *GW*, II, 56 (*Pl*, II, 351).
9. *WBG*, I, 300 - 301 (*Pl*, I, 637); *C*, 151 - 55, 164 - 66, 178 - 81 (*Pl*, III, 116 - 19, 126 - 28, 136 - 39).
10. *WBG*, II, 13 (*Pl*, I, 713).
11. *WBG*, I, 328 (*Pl*, I, 656).
12. *WBG*, I, 308 (*Pl*, I, 643).
13. *WBG*, II, 155 (*Pl*, I, 812).
14. *SW*, 265 (*Pl*, I, 206).
15. *SW*, 268 (*Pl*, I, 208).
16. *SW*, 270 (*Pl*, I, 210).
17. *PR*, 191 (*Pl*, III, 866).
18. *PR*, 204 (*Pl*, III, 878).
19. *WBG*, I, 143 - 50 (*Pl*, I, 529 - 34).
20. *SW*, 264 (*Pl*, I, 209).
21. *SW*, 307 (*Pl*, I, 237).
22. *SW*, 362 (*Pl*, I, 279).
23. Ibid.
24. *SW*, 484 (*Pl*, I, 374).
25. *CP*, I, 252 (*Pl*, II, 781).
26. *PR*, 259 - 60, 382, 402 (*Pl*, III, 926, 1031, 1048).
27. *SW*, 100 (*Pl*, I, 80); *WBG*, II, 259 (*Pl*, I, 886).
28. *WBG*, I, 272 (*Pl*, I, 617 - 18).
29. *WBG*, II, 235 (*Pl*, I, 869).
30. *WBG*, II, 283 - 84. This interest in the genre of "still life" (*nature*

morte) draws a special significance from its relation to the theme of death, so central to the *Recherche* (*WBG*, II, 197 (*Pl*, I, 843)).

Chapter Nine

1. *SW*, 1 (*Pl*, I, 3).
2. *SW*, 47 - 48 (*Pl*, I, 39).
3. *PR*, 225 (*Pl*, III, 895).
4. *PR*, 26 (*Pl*, III, 720).
5. *PR*, 242 (*Pl*, III, 911).
6. *SW*, 91 (*Pl*, I, 74).
7. *SW*, 52 (*Pl*, I, 43).
8. *CP*, I, 302; *C*, 256 (*Pl*, II, 817; III, 192).
9. *SW*, 26 (*Pl*, I, 22 - 23).
10. *SW*, 30, 66 (*Pl*, I, 26, 54).
11. *WBG*, I, 221 (*Pl*, I, 583).
12. *SW*, 220 (*Pl*, I, 171).
13. *PR*, 217 - 18 (*Pl*, III, 889).
14. *SW*, 48 - 49 (*Pl*, I, 40).
15. *SW*, 10 (*Pl*, I, 10).
16. *PR*, 190; *WBG*, I, 202 (*Pl*, III, 866; II, 569).
17. *SW*, 153 - 54 (*Pl*, I, 121).
18. *SW*, 105 (*Pl*, I, 85).
19. *SW*, 248 (*Pl*, I, 193).
20. *PR*, 108 (*Pl*, III, 795).
21. *SCG*, 43 (*Pl*, III, 447).
22. *PR*, 208 (*Pl*, III, 881).
23. *SW*, 188 (*Pl*, I, 146).
24. *SW*, 223 (*Pl*, I, 173).
25. *PR*, 25 (*Pl*, III, 717 - 19).
26. *PR*, 190 (*Pl*, III, 866).
27. *WBG*, I, 323 (*Pl*, I, 653).
28. *CP*, I, 208 (*Pl*, II, 750).
29. *PR*, 229 (*Pl*, III, 899).
30. *SW*, 121 (*Pl*, I, 97).
31. *WBG*, I, 63 - 66 (*Pl*, I, 473 - 75).
32. *WBG*, I, 185 (*Pl*, I, 558).
33. *C*, 348 (*Pl*, III, 258).
34. *C*, 355 (*Pl*, III, 263).
35. *SW*, 229 (*Pl*, I, 178).
36. *C*, 66 (*Pl*, III, 56).
37. *C*, 169 (*Pl*, III, 129).
38. *GW*, II, 153 - 54 (*Pl*, II, 419).
39. *GW*, II, 156 (*Pl*, II, 421).
40. *CP*, II, 123 (*Pl*, II, 943).

41. *C*, 520 (*Pl*, III, 382).
42. *C*, 512 (*Pl*, III, 375).
43. *C*, 352, 511; *PR*, 191 (*Pl*, III, 261, 375, 866).
44. *GW*, II, 153 (*Pl*, II, 419).
45. *C*, 520 (*Pl*, III, 382).
46. *SCG.*, 156 (*Pl*, III, 529).
47. *PR*, 239 - 40 (*Pl*, III, 908).

Chapter Ten

1. *Contre Sainte-Beuve* (Paris: Gallimard, 1954), pp. 157, 165.
2. See, for example, G. Cattaui, *Proust et ses métamorphoses* (Paris: Nizet, 1972).
3. *PR*, 252 - 53 (*Pl*, III, 919 - 20).
4. R. Moser, *L'Impressionnisme français: musique—peinture—littérature* (Genève: Droz, 1952), pp. 141, 147, 132.

Chapter Eleven

1. See P. Brady, "Other-Portrayal and Self-Betrayal in *Manon Lescaut* and *La Vie de Marianne*," *The Romanic Review* 66, no 2 (April, 1973), 99 - 110 and "Deceit and Self-Deceit in *Manon Lescaut* and *La Vie de Marianne*," *Modern Language Review* 72, no 1 (January, 1977), 46 - 52.
2. See P. Brady, "Rococo Style in the Novel: *La Vie de Marianne*," *Studi francesi* 19, no 2 (May - August, 1975), 25 - 43.
3. Another connection: a prominent vein of Kafka criticism sees homosexuality as a central and crucial (if covert) preoccupation of that writer.

Selected Bibliography

PRIMARY SOURCES

1. The masterpiece: *A la recherche du temps perdu*
a. First editions
Du côté de chez Swann. Paris: Grasset, 1913.
A l'ombre des jeunes filles en fleurs. Paris: Nouvelle Revue Française, 1918.
Le côté de Guermantes. Paris: N.R.F., 1920.
Sodome et Gomorrhe. Paris: N.R.F., 1921 and 1922.
La Prisonnière. Paris: N.R.F., 1923.
La Fugitive. Paris: N.R.F., 1925.
Le Temps retrouvé. Paris: N.R.F., 1927.

b. Critical edition
A la recherche du temps perdu. Bibliothèque de la Pléïade. 3 vols. Paris: Gallimard, 1954. Partly unpublished text, established on the handwritten manuscripts; variants, critical apparatus, introduction, summary of each part of the work; index of the names of characters and of place-names; chronology of Marcel Proust by Pierre Clarac and André Ferré; preface by André Maurois.

2. Other works
Portraits de peintre. Paris: Au ménestrel, 1896. Reprinted in *Les Plaisirs et les jours*.
Un amour de Swann. Paris: Gallimard, 1919.
Pastiches et mélanges. Paris: Gallimard, 1919.
La Jalousie. Paris: Fayard, 1921. Complete unpublished novel.
Les Plaisirs et les jours. Preface by Anatole France. Paris: Gallimard, 1924.
Chroniques. Paris: Gallimard, 1927.
Le Balzac de Monsieur de Guermantes. Neuchâtel: Ides et Calendes, 1950.
Jean Santeuil. 3 vols. Paris: Gallimard, 1952.
Contre Sainte-Beuve and *Nouveaux mélanges*. Preface by Bernard de Fallois. Paris: Gallimard, 1954. Reprinted in the Collection "Idées," no. 81 (Paris: Gallimard, 1965).

3. Correspondence
Lettres de Marcel Proust à René Blum, Bernard Grasset et Louis Brun. Collection Classiques du XXe siècle, no. 6. Paris: Kra, 1930.
Lettres de Marcel Proust à la N.R.F. Paris: Gallimard, 1932. Preceded by a bibliography by G. da Silva Ramos.

Lettres de Marcel Proust à Mme C. Preface by Lucien Daudet. Paris: Janin, 1946.

Lettres de Marcel Proust à André Gide. Neuchâtel: Ides et Calendes, 1949.

Correspondance de Marcel Proust avec sa mère. Preface by P. Kolb. Paris: Plon, 1953.

4. Translations and Prefaces

La Bible d'Amiens by John Ruskin. Translated with notes and preface by Marcel Proust. Paris: Mercure de France, 1926.

Sésame et les Lys by John Ruskin. Translated with notes and preface by Marcel Proust. Paris: Mercure de France, 1935.

SECONDARY SOURCES

1. Bibliographies

ZEPHIR, J. J. *La personnalité humaine dans l'oeuvre de Marcel Proust,* Bibliothèque des Lettres modernes, no 1. Paris: Lettres modernes, 1959. Pp. 289 - 323.

CATTAUI, GEORGE. *Proust perdu et retrouvé.* Paris: Plon, 1963. Pp. 199 - 202.

LOWERY, B. *Marcel Proust et Henry James.* Paris: Plon, 1964. Pp. 398 - 412.

"Marcel Proust, Essai de bibliographie." In *Livres de France, Revue littéraire mensuelle* 16, no 5 (May, 1965), 21 - 24. Preceded by a *Chronologie de la vie de Marcel Proust,* pp. 19 - 20.

CLARAC, P., and FERRÉ, A., eds. *Album Proust,* Bibliothèque de la Pléïade. Paris: Gallimard, 1965.

Exposition Proust. Paris: Bibliothèque Nationale, 1965.

PAINTER, GEORGE. *Marcel Proust.* Boston: Little, Brown, 1965. Vol. 2, pp. 365 - 74.

2. Books

BECKETT, SAMUEL. *Proust.* London: Chatto and Windus, 1931; New York: Grove, 1957. Penetrating little study of the theme of time.

BELL, WILLIAM. *Proust's Nocturnal Muse.* New York, 1962. Interesting study of the role of dreams in the *Recherche*—a highly significant and dramatic element.

BERSANI, LEO. *Marcel Proust: The Fictions of Life and of Art.* New York: Oxford University Press, 1965. Basically an intelligent traditional psychological analysis.

BRÉE, GERMAINE. *The World of Marcel Proust.* Boston: Houghton Mifflin, 1966. Penetrating and useful study with a review of previous criticism, by one of the most distinguished specialists.

CAZEAUX, JACQUES. *L'Ecriture de Proust ou l'art du vitrail.* Paris: Gallimard, 1971. Sophisticated work on imagery and the visual—Elstir, Berma, the Guermantes at the Opéra. Modern; slightly obscure, but evocative. Strongly recommended.

CHANTAL, RENÉ DE. *Marcel Proust critique littéraire.* 2 vols. Montréal: Presses de l'Université de Montréal 1967. Important because of the central importance of Proust's conceptions of criticism and literature in the *Recherche.* Thorough study.

DELEUZE, GILLES. *Proust et les signes.* Paris: Presses Universities de France, 1971. Excellent elucidation of the several levels of signs in the *Recherche:* social signs (empty), signs of love (deceptive), sensory signs (material), and signs of art (essential). Unfortunately confuses the narrator with Proust.

DOUBROVSKY, SERGE. *La Place de la Madeleine.* Paris: Mercure de France, 1974. Brilliant if unconvincing attempt to show the narrator (identified with Proust—as is the *petite madeleine,*-P.M.,- Proust Marcel) as desirous of eliminating his mother (she also identified with the *madeleine*) through ingestion and defecation. Provocative.

FLORIVAL, G. *Le Désir chez Proust.* Paris: Nauwelaerts, 1971. Penetrating psychoanalytical study, based on Freud and Lacan. Strongly recommended. Not for the uninitiated reader.

GENETTE, GÉRARD. *Figures III.* Paris: Seuil, 1972. Somewhat technical but highly competent structural analysis of the *Recherche* from a stylistic point of view, with special attention to the place and function of methaphor and metonymy.

LESAGE, LAURENT. *Marcel Proust and His Literary Friends.* Urbana,Ill.: U. of Illinois Press, 1958. Interesting collection of essays on Proust's relations with his contemporaries, not all of whom turn out to be "friends."

MOUTON, JEAN. *Le Style de Marcel Proust.* Paris: Corrêa, 1948. Valuable stylistic study of a traditional bent.

MULLER, MARCEL. *Les Voix narratives dans "A la recherche du temps perdu."* Genève: Droz, 1965. Essential work on point of view, so central to an understanding of the true status of the discourse of the *Recherche.*

PAINTER, GEORGE. *Proust.* 2 vols. Boston: Little, Brown, 1959 - 1965. The standard biography of Proust. Fascinating reading. Unfortunately unscientific and anecdotal. Fallaciously argues (in flagrant contradiction of Proust's own view) that the *Recherche* cannot be understood without recourse to Proust's life, the *Recherche* being thus seen as not really fiction at all but autobiography. The status of Painter's biography is invalidated by the unscholarly introduction of fictional passages from the *Recherche.* In Painter, Proust has found his nemesis: a posthumous Sainte-Beuve.

PEYRE, HENRI. *Marcel Proust.* New York: Columbia University Press, 1970. Admirable general study in a traditional vein by the well-known authority on French literature.

POULET, GEORGES. *L'Espace proustien.* Paris: Gallimard, 1963. One of the better studies by Poulet, less marred than others by the quotation of passages out of context. Distinguishes Proust's viewpoint from that of Bergson.

RICHARD, JEAN-PIERRE. *Proust et le monde sensible.* Paris: Seuil, 1974. Brilliant study. Emphasizes the interrelationship between the various volumes (denied by Poulet and others).

SHATTUCK, ROGER. *Proust's Binoculars: A Study of Memory, Time, and Recognition in "A la recherche du temps perdu."* New York: Random House, 1963. Valuable work on imagery and above all on the question of vision.

TADIÉ, YVES. *Proust et le roman: Essai sur les formes et techniques du roman dans "A la recherche du temps perdu."* Paris: Gallimard, 1971. Recent, essential work on the *Recherche*—a most competent and comprehensive investigation.

VAN DE GHINSTE, J. *Rapports humains et communication dans "A la recherche du temps perdu."* Paris: Nizet, 1975. Interesting and valuable study of the *Recherche* from an important point of view.

ZIMA, P.-V. *Le Désir du mythe: Un lecture sociologique de Marcel Proust.* Paris: Nizet, 1973. Valuable attempt to apply to the Proustian opus the socio-critical perspective ("genetic structuralism") of Lucien Goldmann.

3. Articles

BILEN, M. "L'univers mythique de Marcel Proust." In *Dialectique créatrice et structure de l'oeuvre littéraire.* Paris: Vrin, 1971. The important archetypal intuition suggested in the title is soon forgotten in this interesting but traditional and ultimately disappointing study.

BRADY, P. "Farms, Trees, and Bell-Towers: The 'Hidden Meaning' of Triads in *A la recherche du temps perdu.*" *Neophilologus*, vol. LXI, no 3 (July 1977), pp. 371 - 377. An attempt to go beyond previous interpretations (including that proposed by the fictional narrator) of the centrally important element of the three bell-towers, their "hidden meaning," and the strange pleasure it causes.

GIRARD, R. "Les mondes proustiens." In *Mensonge romantique et vérité romanesque.* Paris: Grasset, 1961. Perceptive application of Girard's concept of mediation: whereas Combray is united by love of self and respect for Aunt Léonie, the Verdurin salon is united by secret adoration of the absent and exclusive Guermantes, a consequent assumption and declaration of hatred of those "ennuyeux," and a contempt for self which finds expression in spiteful treatment of a Saniette.

LEVIN, H. "Marcel Proust." In *The Gates of Horn.* New York: Oxford University Press, 1966. Distinguished classical essay. A salutory warning against reductive interpretations of the *Recherche* based on simply reading the female partners (Albertine, Andrée) as males. Emphasis on the *Recherche* as means of initiation and of maturation for the reader.

MARTIN-CHAUFFIER, L. "Proust et le double 'je' de quatre personnes." *Confluences* 3 (July - August, 1943), 55 - 69. Valuable essay on the problem of point of view.

MEHLMANN, G. *A Structural Study of Autobiography.* Ithaca: Cornell University Press, 1974. Suggestive Lacanian study, stressing identification of narrator with Aunt Léonie, and marred only by confusion of narrator with Proust.

ORTEGA Y GASSET, JOSÉ. "Le temps, la distance, et la forme chez Marcel Proust." *Les Cahiers Marcel Proust* 1 (1927), pp. 287 - 299. Useful study of certain formal-philosophical categories in Proust.

Index